MW00440002

TRUE COMMITMENTS

TRUE COMMITMENTS

a memoir

DID YOU THINK THE WAR WAS OVER

TIGER CAGE VIGIL & FAST for PEACE in INDOCHINA

MICHAEL TRUE

Haley's

Athol, Massachusetts

Manuscript digitized by Debra Ellis.

Copy edited by Eveline MacDougall. Proof read by Richard Bruno.

Special thanks to Claire Schaeffer-Duffy for exhaustive attention to fact and detail during prepublication review.

Photos from the collection of the estate of Michael True unless otherwise credited.

Haley's
488 South Main Street
Athol, MA 01331
haley.antique@verizon.net

Library of Congress Cataloging-in-Publication Data
Names: True, Michael, 1933- author.
Title: True commitments : a memoir / Michael True.
Description: Athol, Massachusetts : Haley's, [2020] | Summary: "Michael
    True, late professor emeritus of literature and peace studies, relates
    his experiences with literature, religion, and nonviolence in
    Massachusetts and later in Europe, Asia, and Latin America. His six
    adult children provide separate perspectives on their father's life"--
    Provided by publisher.
Identifiers: LCCN 2020036269 (print) | LCCN 2020036270 (ebook) |
ISBN
    9781948380379 (trade paperback) | ISBN 9781948380386 (hardcover)
| ISBN
    9781948380393 (epub)
Subjects: LCSH: True, Michael, 1933- | Nonviolence. | Peace--Study and
    teaching.
Classification: LCC HM1281 .T78 2020 (print) | LCC HM1281
(ebook) | DDC
    303.6//1092 [B]--dc23
LC record available at https://lccn.loc.gov/2020036269
LC ebook record available at https://lccn.loc.gov/2020036270

Those we love become part of who we are.
And when they leave this world,
their love stays with us always.

—source unknown

Contents

Illustrations ix

Energy, Generosity, and Happiest in Motion
   a preface by Betsy True xi

Precious Characteristics
   a foreword by Scott Schaeffer-Duffy xv

Life: "a remarkable pilgrimage"
   a foreword by Claire Schaeffer-Duffy xvii

A Centripetal Force Moving Me toward Who I Am 1

Oklahoma, 1933 3

Minnesota, North Carolina, Indiana, 1955 30

Massachusetts, 1965 46

England and Western Europe 82

Manifesto 91

Anniversary 91

China and Korea 95

Back Home 116

India and Latin America 129

Who I Will Be Being 151

Michael's Children Remember Him 153

   A Life Well Lived by Mary Laurel True 155

   No Interest in Some Things by Michael True 157

   "Use Your Imagination." by John True 160

   A Love of Culture by Christopher True 162

   Grateful for His Life by Anne True 164

   Essence of His Spirit by Betsy True 167

About the Author 171
Acknowledgments. 173
Colophon. 175

Illustrations

Michael's father, Guy Herbert True 5

Michael's paternal family 8

Michael's maternal family 10

Michael's mother and her sister 11

Michael with his parents 17

Michael with friends 21

Michael in Army ROTC 28

Michael and Mary Pat Delaney on their wedding day 35

Michael at Assumption College 47

Mary Pat and Michael with their family, about 1967 48

Daniel Berrigan and Michael 50

Robert Bly with Michael 52

Dorothy Day and Roland Werme 57

Floating Parish of Worcester 60

Floating Parish brochure 61

general procedures of the Floating Parish 62

Michael and Jim Noonan protest the Vietnam War 65

Robert Bly and Michael 66

invitation to 1974 appearance of Denise Levertov 67

1973-1974 Worcester Poetry Festival brochure 68

a protest cartoon from Michael's collection 74

1978 Upper Midwest Writers Conference brochure 76

Michael's Nanjing colleagues 97

1989 Nanjing protest 106

North Korean colleagues and Michael in Pyongyang 112

protesters including Michael at GTE plant 118

Joe Egger, Michael, and Colman McCarthy....................119
Michael at School of the Americas civil disobedience action.....120
Michael and Mary Pat with colleagues in Hawaii...............125
Michael aboard an elephant in Jaipur, India....................136
Michael with Pratibha Patil, president of India.................140
Michael and Mary Pat's children in August 2014...............152
letter to Michael from US Representative Jim McGovern.......154

Energy, Generosity, and Happiest in Motion

a preface by Betsy True, Michael's daughter

In his memoir, my father recounts in great detail his childhood in Oklahoma with his parents, grandparents, and his beloved brothers. My father also writes about his formative school years and later college and graduate school. He also writes about years of teaching college in the US and in England, China, India, and many other countries. I appreciate his stories, but I found myself wanting to learn more about his personal rather than professional life and affiliations.

What I remember most about my father is his energy, his generosity, and his endless drive. He loved welcoming people into our house, especially at Christmas and Easter. Our parents made every gathering a celebration, a chance to be with friends and family in our old, "comfortable and handsome" (my father's words) house, near Elm Park in Worcester, Massachusetts. When guests arrived, my father waved his hands and exclaimed, "Hey, isn't this great?"

On hot summer days, my father took us to Indian Lake, Rutland State Park, or the Bennett Field swimming pool. He loved summer heat, but even more, he loved being near water. We sometimes stayed in Ogunquit, Maine, in an old house on a windy road near Perkins Cove. And without tiring, he walked for miles on the beach.

My father seemed happiest when he was in motion—paddling around in a pool, walking to or from the bus (a family of eight, we had just one—usually unreliable—used car for all of us) or to the grocery store. In later years, my father took water aerobics classes at Quinsigamond Community College and the YWCA in downtown Worcester. Marveling that he was often the only man in class, he made friends with those in the pool. My father committed himself wholeheartedly to an exercise routine. After water aerobics, he went for coffee at Crown Bakery, Bagel Time, or Espress Yourself before heading to his home office to write.

When I was younger, my father's speed walking frustrated me, as I couldn't keep up with his pace. He moved quickly, rushing to the post office or to the downtown library. When he did relax, it was usually to talk with someone at our kitchen table. With the tea kettle going and box of Entenmann's sweet rolls, my father welcomed whoever might stop by to chat. It never ceases to amaze me how many friends sought my father's counsel. He had a depth of knowledge for people and places far and wide. And as a way to help them with whatever they needed, he offered people his personal connections including phone numbers and addresses.

When the telephone rang on a table under the stairwell, my father would answer it and get lost in deep conversation. Then the doorbell rang and another friend joined the kitchen's round table discussion. For years, my parents left our front door unlocked at all times. And except for a stolen bike, nothing was ever taken from inside or outside the house.

After taking a daily break for coffee, my father retreated to his office on the second floor and began furiously typing, first on an old typewriter, then on an IBM electric, and later on a desktop computer. He always had a letter to the editor, essay, or book review to write. And if there were any doubt of his productivity, when we went through his old filing cabinet in February of 2019, we found four long drawers filled with fifty years of correspondence between my father and poets, writers, peace activists, book publishers, colleagues, and friends from around the world. He made connections with people that lasted a lifetime.

Not long before my father died, we had an impromptu farewell party at Goddard House as my parents planned to move from Worcester—their home of fifty-five years—to an assisted living facility in Minneapolis. Despite the short notice, more than forty people came to say goodbye. My twin sister, Anne, asked people to introduce themselves and tell what year they met my father. "I first met Mike . . . in 1967 . . . or 1970 . . . 1975." So many people had known my father for decades.

I remember rituals we had growing up.

Every evening after work, at approximately 4:30 pm, my parents had their own happy hour, a Manhattan for my mother and Schlitz or Pabst Blue Ribbon for my father with cheese and crackers, dry-roasted peanuts, or Fritos. We kids weren't invited when my parents reviewed their day unless someone happened to stop by for a visit. Then we could join the discussion.

On Friday nights, we ordered pizza from Jason's on June Street. We always ordered four to ensure our fifth pizza was free. If my parents wanted to celebrate, we went with them to the White House on Park Avenue to feast on whipped cheese and crackers. My father also favored that restaurant for entertaining visiting poets and writers before a reading at Assumption College, where he taught, or the public library.

On Saturdays, my siblings and I were expected to clean the house. My mother had a list of chores and usually cleverly titled it with an S allitera-tion, such as Saturday Sludge, when we signed up for a half hour of cleaning a room, vacuuming rugs, washing windows, or dusting. My father often made dinner on Saturdays: hamburgers, chocolate shakes, and French fries.

Our childhood home often felt chaotic because of the number of people living there. Even so, my family often had visitors—friends, neighbors, schoolmates, relatives.

My mother and father brought order to our lives by showing us how to live every day with purpose. We knew that, by engaging with visitors to the family, we built a larger community. Among the many visitors to our home, I met peace activists, writers, and poets who reached a wide audience. People stayed with us from all over the country and all over the world. They gave me a sense that their actions and words created hope and energy.

With my father's death, our community—and, thus, my community—has shrunk. He was a conduit for so many people to meet. I'm lucky to have the memories of childhood filled with interesting people. Recently, one of my friends and I discussed the power of place and, specifically, the power of home.

My father's Worcester home grounded him. There, he gathered with us for the Floating Parish on Sunday mornings, with my mother and friends or colleagues for dinner parties they hosted, or with people in social justice groups. When the family house sold in 2015, I think he and we all lost some of our bearings. Our gathering place had disappeared. I wonder what it was like for my parents, who had lived in the same house for all of those years to move, then, in their eighties, to a new locale.

I'm grateful for my father's life and the memories he gave me and all of us. My father was a great teacher. His determined, lively spirit will always inspire me. I hope it will inspire everyone who reads this memoir.

Marginal Way, Ogunquit, Maine, where the True family sometimes vacationed.

Precious Characteristics
a preface by Scott Schaeffer-Duffy

In our nearly four decades in the Catholic Worker movement, we have met many extraordinary people: activists, academics, artists, authors, actors, poets, bishops, priests, women religious, musicians, workers, parents, grandparents, and children. Some were renowned, others known only to a few people. Some were wealthy, others dirt-poor. Each had unique gifts and special wisdom to share. Some became dear friends.

In many ways, Michael True possessed a greater variety of precious characteristics than anyone else we were blessed to meet. A professor of English who never treated us as intellectual inferiors, a parent who never lectured us on how to raise our four children, a benefactor who rescued us and our community countless times, a resident of Worcester's affluent West Side yet one of few overnight visitors we had in Saint Benedict's Catholic Worker in a Washington, DC neighborhood where few outsiders dared visit us even during the day, a person older than us by many years who treated us nonetheless as equals, a passionate voice for justice and peace, Michael True was a treasure, an invaluable ally and friend.

A friend of the Catholic Worker co-founder Dorothy Day, peacemakers including Daniel Berrigan, and poets of the caliber of Stanley Kunitz, Michael introduced us to the giants of his generation. Unlike some academics who merely shed light on actions of others, he invited us and many to speak about peace to his classes. He helped organize New England Catholic Peace Fellowship conferences. When we were on trial for opposing nuclear weapons and the Gulf War, he gave expert testimony in court on the historical effectiveness of civil disobedience. He braved wind, heat, cold, snow, and rain as a faithful participant in Worcester's weekly peace vigil. He refused to pay war taxes and even got arrested with us to oppose the MX nuclear missile. He traveled more than once to India to tap into the wisdom of Gandhians, Jains, Hindus, and Buddhists.

Despite more than five decades opposing the horrors of war, he never lost his sense of humor.

When I once mentioned humility, Michael, one of the most modest people I ever met, joked, "Humility is for those with nothing to brag about."

His face lit up when he laughed. I can still feel the hope inherent in his sense of humor. His death greatly diminished our lives. He was so steadfast that Claire and I were seduced into believing he would live forever.

I hope and pray that his writings will preserve Michael True as the gift he was to us and to humanity.

Life: "a remarkable pilgrimage"
a foreword by Claire Schaeffer-Duffy

I met Michael when I was a young Catholic Worker in Washington, DC. It was the early 1980s, the era of Reaganomics, a time when the country invested huge sums of money to enlarge its nuclear arsenal, when crack decimated inner-city neighborhoods, and nearly two thousand homeless people slept on the streets of the nation's capital.

The national scene could have caused some to despair. Not Michael. The professor of English from Massachusetts had come to Washington to give his slide presentation, "The American Tradition of Nonviolence." The venue? A squalid Catholic Worker house on Fourth Street NW crowded with people and the occasional rat.

Typical of him, he did not want merely to lecture on nonviolence. The next day, he joined our weekly protest at a local nuclear weapons facility. I can still see him with collared shirt and tie in the back seat of our hazardous Ford van as he looked downright giddy among a band of scruffy Catholic Workers off to denounce the madness of a national security policy based on mutually assured destruction.

"I lived by the seat of my pants," Michael once told me in his later years. That modest summary, as his memoir reveals, belies the rich coherence underlying his life. Unafraid to evolve, he trusted his passions and took seriously his curiosities—way leading on to way. In that, he embodied the immeasurable value of a liberal arts education with its emphasis on inquiry. He embodied, too, the animating joy and vitality of determining what you believe and trying to live by it. As Michael notes in *True Commitments*, life can indeed be "a remarkable pilgrimage, a frequent setting out in a leaky boat."

Despite setbacks and wrong turns, Michael's pilgrimage was quite marvelous. The Depression-era boy from a conservative town in Oklahoma—who loved math and read little more than geography magazines—went on to become a professor of American literature, prolific writer, tax resister, and peace scholar who taught and traveled widely.

I leave to others more well-versed than me to review Michael's achievements as literary critic and professor of literature. I knew him best as advocate and scholar of nonviolence. Yet, literature and peace, two major orientations in his life, were never disconnected from each other. Writers he studied and loved—poets Wilfred Owens, Denise Levertov, and essayist Randall Bourne, to name very few—awakened his consciousness to a more humane way of living while the peacemakers gave example.

Like so many people who regard the peaceable kin-dom as an achievable reality rather than mere vision, Michael fought against the cynicism that tolerates mass slaughter and critics who dismiss peace studies as a flimsy discipline. He well knew we live in a killing world. He knew that empire and violence define US history. He also knew that alongside exploitation and massacres occur accounts of war resisters, abolitionists, labor organizers, and others who gave their lives to building more just and human-centered arrangements. Michael devoted much intellectual energy to illuminating *their* stories.

Of the thirteen books he authored or co-edited, eight have peacemaking and nonviolence as their theme. Two profile the lives of peacemakers and their communities. Other works look at peacemaking in the context of family life. One explores the nonviolent tradition in American literature. In the book's introduction, Michael acknowledges nonviolence as one American literary tradition among many, its path sometimes "wiggly and overgrown" but distinctively there nonetheless.

Peace studies was an emerging academic field when Michael entered it. An energetic champion of its development, he promulgated the pioneering work of peace researchers Elise and Kenneth Boulding, Johan Galtung, and Gene Sharp. He held leadership positions in the International Peace

Research Association and its American counterpart, Consortium on Peace Research and Education. He contributed to articulation of the United Nations Culture of Peace Program and its provision of a robust and practical template for constructing "positive peace."

Small wonder that poets and peacemakers, both peoples of unconventional expression, would attract Michael. A desire to find an "appropriate language that sustains us and for social change" animated much of his work. For him, the poets had the last say. During his final, enfeebling months, he kept *The Collected Poems of Denise Levertov* by his bedside. He loved her poem "Making Peace," which likens the work of peace to the process of writing a poem. It concludes:

> A cadence of peace might balance its weight
> on that different fulcrum; peace, a presence,
> an energy field more intense than war,
> might pulse then,
> stanza by stanza into the world,
> each act of living
> one of its words, each word
> a vibration of light—facets
> of the forming crystal.

Levertov's words could well apply to Michael. The man who worked to make visible the unseen currents of peace himself flowed with it, his life a pulsing stanza that energized many.

I am so glad that my dear friend, a prolific profiler, found time to tell his own story.

A Centripetal Force Moving Me toward Who I Am

an introduction by Michael True

Anyone has a nerve writing an autobiography, rightly regarded as the supreme egotistical act. Not writing it, letting all that life and all those people disappear without some remembrance and appreciation, however, seems wasteful.

At times, I came to wonder if there is any such thing as the self, that elusive entity one is forever misplacing, then reclaiming, across a changing landscape. Other people, of course, including the Buddha, had something to say about that, as did Pablo Neruda:

> Of the many men whom I am, whom we are
> I can not settle on a single one.
> They are lost to me under cover of clothing.
> They have departed for another city.

Along the way, nevertheless, a recognizable person emerged, and some principle being revealed itself "from which I struggled not to stray," to borrow the words of the poet Stanley Kunitz.

I think of my life not as a journey, since that sounds too linear, but as an unfolding as I threw myself into whatever came along—new places, happenings, unexpected events, personal encounters: a centripetal force moving me toward who I am.

Acknowledging encounters and identifying points in time, I am rather unsure of their meaning. My hope is that any reader who happens along may come across experiences that resonate with one's own.

Oklahoma, 1933

Wherever we looked, the land would hold us up.

—William Stafford

As for being born: that happened at St. Anthony's Hospital, Oklahoma City, on November 8, 1933, the year that unemployment hit twenty-five percent. My dad was traveling, selling auto parts, fuel pumps, gaskets, that sort of thing. My mother knew he was out of town at the time, in fact planned it that way.

"Herbert," she said."Now you leave me at Mama's and go back to the road. I don't want you around walking the floor for days—you know from the other two boys, I'll be slow. If it's a girl, I'll call the highway patrol, perhaps somewhere between Woodword and Altus or wherever and tell them to stop you if they can." Although that moment was a fixed point in time, I carried the legacy of previous travelers in my bones.

My paternal grandmother, Mary Elizabeth Bottomley True, had moved from Newburyport, Massachusetts, to Minnesota and from there to Oklahoma in 1912. Although born in Massachusetts, both paternal grandparents had moved with their respective families to southern Minnesota shortly after the Civil War. The father of my paternal grandfather, J. W. True, a Civil War veteran whose ancestors arrived in the American colonies about 1640, qualified for help in obtaining a farm in Truman, Minnesota. Similarly, my grandmother had settled with her family near Winnebago, another small town in southern Minnesota.

Lizzy, as her husband (my grandfather) called her, and J. W. True had met at Mankato State Normal School. After graduating in 1893, they married and lived on High Street across from what became Minnesota State University at Mankato. There, their five children were born: Laurel

3

May, Guy Herbert (my father, born on November 1, 1896), Jay Wesley Jr. (Jamie), Jeannette, and Charles. Grandfather True's printing business, which included the Mankota Free Press, was relatively successful. His travels took him throughout the region and to the Upper Midwest.

Because my grandfather "had endured Minnesota winters long enough by 1912" and with the encouragement of friends and the promise of warmer weather, he, my grandmother, and their five children left Mankato for Oklahoma City. When they arrived in the capital of the new state, then only five years old, the city had a population of about ten thousand people.

Soon after Lizzy arrived in Oklahoma City, she co-founded the Pierian Club, a literary association that took its title from Alexander Pope's verse: "A little learning is a dangerous thing: Drink deep or taste not the Pierian spring." In Greek mythology, the Pierian spring was sacred to the Muses. As her father's copy of Shakespeare's plays suggests, she was interested in literature and politics. Her pince-nez spectacles attached to her blouse, she read the daily newspaper and, at seventy-five, studied Spanish for the first time.

J. W.'s printing business continued successfully in Oklahoma and enabled him to purchase stock in an oil and gas company that provided well for his widow after he died in 1932. All five children attended college, although only the two women graduated, Laurel in English in 1915 and Jeannette in music in 1919, both from the University of Oklahoma, Norman. Jamie and Charles eventually went into the oil business, while Herbert, my father, went on a basketball scholarship to the University of Missouri, Columbia.

During the spring semester, however, after the US entered World War I, he and two of his buddies drove to Kansas City to enlist in the army. Not surprisingly, my grandfather took the train from Oklahoma City to Kansas City as soon as he got the news that his twenty-year-old son had signed up. Shortly afterward, the 35th Division, mostly from Oklahoma, Kansas, and Missouri and later under the command of Harry S Truman, was assigned to Fort Sill, Oklahoma, eighty miles from Oklahoma City. So the family saw him often before he left for the Western Front.

About a year before the war ended, my father was gassed in the Argonne Forest in a major offensive involving American forces. Fortunately, his army buddy carried him in a blanket to a battle station for treatment, or I wouldn't be around to tell his story. Because of his injury, doctors recommended that he enter a sanitarium after he returned home. Instead, he promised to spend a lot of time outdoors, so his job took him on the road rather than into an office.

As he walked down Main Street shortly after returning from France, he recognized a young woman, Agnes Murphy, walking in the opposite direction. After passing one another, both turned around, then smiled. A few months later, my father—already a salesman traveling to outlying

Michael's father, Guy Herbert True, during World War I

towns—proposed to her. They agreed to run away to get married. They planned for Agnes to meet him in El Reno, twenty miles west of the city, to be married by a Catholic priest.

Agnes took the inner-urban, a glorified street car, to El Reno on November 29, 1919. She was prepared to return by the same car if Herbert wasn't at the station to meet her.

He was there.

5

Years later, my brothers and I discovered, upon reading their marriage certificate, that a Methodist Episcopal clergyman married them. The Catholic priest refused to marry them because they hadn't had pre-Cana, or pre-marriage, instruction prior to the wedding. When, at sixty, my mother owned up to the so-called scandal, my ornery older brother questioned her. "So, Mother. Were you pregnant?"

She answered, "I was not." The Protestant ceremony weighed on her conscience, so they later had the marriage "blessed" by a Catholic priest at St. Anthony's parish in Oklahoma City.

For different reasons, their runaway marriage shocked both sets of parents. The Trues were Protestant, traditionally Unitarians or Presbyterians, while my maternal grandparents, the Murphys, were Roman Catholic. The first time my father brought his "Roman" bride to his parents' home, Grandmother True took her youngest child, Jeannette, and hid in an upstairs closet. The working class Murphys lived less than a mile from the upper middle-class, well-educated Trues.

Overwhelmed by the True family scene—children, spouses, other comparatively wealthy and sophisticated relatives—my mother fainted at the Thanksgiving dinner table. In time, nonetheless, she won her mother-in-law's respect, and they became good friends. Both were strong, intelligent, and independent, however different in background and experience. When my mother learned to play bridge, a popular after-dinner pastime among the Trues, she proved herself astute at the game.

Grandmother True spent one afternoon a week mending clothes with her church group for people living in Walnut Grove, a settlement near the North Canadian River bed south of Oklahoma City. When the family gathered at her home at Christmas or on her birthday, she sat at the end of a long, beautifully appointed dinner table, occasionally ringing a dinner bell for the uniformed maid to pass rolls or a second serving to assembled family members. She and my Aunt Jeannette, who taught piano in her studio in their home, were both excellent cooks. Happy memories of our visits include sitting between my father and Uncle Charles in the breakfast nook as they talked politics over breakfast and feasted on leftover biscuits or desserts from the night before.

Fond of my grandparents on both sides of the family, I am a combination of their inheritances and grateful for that: the Irish, Catholic, working-class Murphys and the English, Protestant, middle-class Trues. As a child, I relate more to the True side of the family, particularly Grandmother True, whose influence persists and remains telling. A portrait in our dining room of her at seventy reveals something of her personality. Her gaze steady but gentle, she sits composed with perfect posture in a French provincial chair, reading material in her lap. She has well-groomed white hair and her pince-nez pinned to the left shoulder of her well-tailored suit. As a child visiting her upstairs bedroom, I often found her sorting through newspaper clippings on her white bedspread in order to write her Congressman about some issue. Senator A. S. "Mike" Monroney, an Oklahoma Democrat, was a family friend.

Grandmother True admired Franklin Roosevelt, so when the family gathered in a circle for conversation after dinner, she strongly defended him against the criticism of her more conservative son and son-in-law in the oil business.

At eighty-three, she made the hundred-mile trip on a Southwestern Trailways Bus from Oklahoma City to Lawton, where my family lived, to attend my high school graduation. She and the local newspaper, with my picture on the front page, arrived in the bus station at the same moment. In a graduating class of eleven at St. Mary's Catholic High School, I was valedictorian and Flora Landoll, my classmate for all twelve years, salutatorian.

My industrious, energetic Grandmother Murphy—no less intelligent than Grandmother True—had little formal education. Born Lottie Missouri Walters in West Virginia in the 1870s, she grew up in Nebraska and the Oklahoma Territory before statehood. Her family homestead was near Cashion, north of Oklahoma City. Her parents, ne'er-do-well farmers, had made their way by covered wagon to Nebraska, then south to the banks of the Cimarron River. Later, several family members settled in

*Mary Elizabeth Bottomley, Michael's paternal grandmother; Charles Bottomley,
and Jay Wesley True, Michael's paternal grandfather, from left front;
Laurel May True, unknown man, Guy Herbert True, Michael's father;
Jay Wesley True Jr., Michael's uncle, and Helen Jeanette True, Michael's aunt
from left, back*

the southwestern part of the state near the Wichita Mountains in what
had been a Kiowa-Comanche-Apache reservation. I have often wondered
how, with little money, they managed to care for a large family while
farming in the dry, red soil during hot Oklahoma summers.

The oldest of eight children, Grandmother Murphy lost all but twenty percent of her hearing as a result of a childhood illness. My mother received her first paycheck and bought Grandmother her first hearing aid when Grandmother was forty. Even without the hearing aid, by reading lips she missed very little of what was said in her presence. She met my grandfather, Michael Daniel Murphy, when he and his younger brother, the oldest of nine children, moved south from Fall City, Nebraska, soon after "the Run," when Oklahoma Territory was opened for settlement just after Lottie's family claimed a nearby lot. Grandfather Murphy, for whom I was named, loved to tell about Lottie Missouri Walters, or Sourrie, as he called her, papering the bare walls of his small sod hut before they were married.

Sourrie and Dan, as he was known, were married in a one-room Catholic church in Lockridge, an Irish settlement of O'Briens, O'Connors, and Murphys where Logan, Oklahoma, and Cimarron counties converged. My mother was born there on September 16, 1897, the older of their two daughters. When Dan, who played the fiddle, was forty and my Aunt Lola, three, he gave up booze, took the pledge, and never touched another drop.

I owe to the Murphys my populist sympathies as well as genes for good health and my thick Irish neck. After farming near Lockridge and one year in Western Nebraska, they moved in 1910 to Oklahoma City, where my grandfather owned a team of horses that he hired out to the city. Later, he took a job as janitor at a public elementary school a mile north of the state capital. I loved visiting his basement office in the boiler room, sitting in his big, brown rocking chair, and making the rounds with him as he mended fences, fed goldfish, and mowed the lawn surrounding the schoolhouse. He and my grandmother had an oil well in their backyard, which earned them a small pension—only a pittance of the money it must have earned for the British-American Oil Company.

They lived in three rooms, rented out three rooms on the other side of the house, and kept an icebox on the back porch near a large barrel to catch rainwater.

Margaret Walters Maxwell, Michael's maternal grandmother;
baby Lola Maxwell Murphy; Michael's mother, Agnes Loretta Murphy (later True)
holding Lola; and Lottie Missouri Murphy, Michael's maternal grandmother
from left, front; Elijah Walters, Michael's maternal great-grandfather, and
Michael David Murphy, Michael's maternal grandfather, from left, back

Grandmother was famous for "quick lunches" and what she called a lazy-daisy cake, which she prepared when any of us arrived, day or night. When I stayed with my grandparents, we rode around town or out to the country to visit my cousin H. M. in my grandparents' 1939 black Plymouth sedan. At the end of my visit, with Grandfather Murphy at the wheel, we made the three-hour drive home to Lawton, stopping under a shade tree just off the highway to eat a lunch Grandmother had prepared for us.

Through eighth grade, my mother attended St. Joseph's School, across from the later site of the Alfred P. Murrah Federal Building, destroyed by Timothy McVeigh in the 1995 Oklahoma City bombing. The Sisters of Mercy taught at St. Joseph. Soon afterward, on completing

Michael's mom,
Agnes Murphy True, in 1905, left;
with her sister Lola in 1905,
and in 1915, below

business college, she worked as a secretary in city offices. Her spoken language, rich and imagistic, was livelier than the speech of her sophisticated inlaws. She didn't work outside the home while she raised us. After my older brothers had grown and I was in high school, she worked as a secretary/accountant for the American Red Cross and later as a saleswoman at a feed store. She loved having money of her own and dealing with the public, particularly farmers.

My mother's Catholicism was essential to her identity, and she remained faithful to her religion at considerable cost to herself when she married into a staunch Protestant family. Even though she was anemic and therefore had a priest's dispensation before Vatican II to forego abstinence from meat on Fridays and other prescribed days, she ignored her doctor's orders for fear of causing scandal among her non-Catholic friends. My older brothers and I were dutifully baptized at birth, attended Catholic schools, were married in the Church, and remain grateful beneficiaries of our mother's prayers and her devotion to the rosary. My father recognized the significance of Mother's persistence in the faith and, in tribute to her, became a Catholic after his mother died.

Like many young people growing up anywhere in the United States, I assumed nothing ever happened where we grew up. It was only after I left home that I learned about the early populist history of the Oklahoma City region, reflected in the songs of another native Okie, Woody Guthrie, and about native American history, particularly Geronimo, who died in a Fort Sill prison near Lawton.

Until I was five, we lived at 712 Bell Avenue near the center of town, then moved to an imposing, brown-stained, two-story house on a gravel road about a mile from downtown. Our so-called new home had been neglected for years, one reason my parents could afford it. My mother repaired and redecorated the house inside and out and reclaimed the 75-by-150-foot lot around it. During periodic redecorating sessions with three close friends, she spent hours standing on a wobbly board strung between two ladders as she painted the high walls and ceilings. On the lookout for bargains, she carpeted the living and dining rooms, stairway, and three upstairs bedrooms with handsome floor covering disposed of by Oklahoma City's Skirvin Tower Hotel.

She soon turned the home into a handsome residence in a neighborhood of modest bungalows. One summer afternoon, a moving truck arrived with twin beds for my older brothers and a washing machine filled with boxes of washing-powder gifts from my Grandmother True. Before that, my mother spent hours carrying baskets of dirty clothes to a laundromat, where she washed them and then loaded wet clothes in baskets into the trunk of the car to transport them back to hang on the clothesline before ironing sheets and pillowcases on a mangle, or large ironing machine, in the kitchen.

Oklahoma summers brought periodic droughts with water rationing. Still, my mother and I carried water in a washtub to a circular bed of marigolds, rectangular beds of zinnias, rose bushes, and yellow and purple irises near mulberry trees in the side and back yards. My poem commemorates her gardening.

Her Word
She often talked to flowers:
at seventy-two, she commanded
bougainvillea into bloom.

Oklahoma watched, skeptical
       resentful.

Taking dust and clay,
she willed them into magnolia blossoms,
pampered them into violets,
saying,
"I'm Agnes Murphy: now listen!"
And they did, profusely—
geraniums,
   irises,
     marigolds—
       even dandelions.

She raised a few chickens as well as a pet Canada goose named Jackie, a favorite of my Grandfather Murphy. Jackie occasionally took flight if we forgot to clip one wing to keep him in our yard, but he always returned.

Mrs. Yarwood owned the house next door to us. I never knew her first name. When Mrs. Yarwood died, my grandparents purchased her house, eventually a temporary home for young couples stationed at Fort Sill during the Second World War. Many of them, like Mrs. Yarwood, would hail from exotic locales: back East, out West, or abroad. Along with my early interest in geography, becoming acquainted with them undoubtedly had something to do with my later travels.

Since my family lived some distance from many of my classmates at St. Mary's School or other friends, I spent a lot of time alone or among the few children living nearby, though they were never quite friends in the same sense. That we often got into mischief when we played complicated the divide. One summer afternoon when I was about six, James McMillan and I decided to throw rocks at the few cars driving by on the dirt road separating our houses, which horrified our parents.

Another time, James initiated me into the fascinating, guilty pleasure of taking off all our clothes and experimenting with the mysteries of our body parts. Later, I realized that James may have been sexually molested by a boarder, a thin, gawky man of about thirty. He rented a room in the McMillans' small house and rode to and from work on a bicycle. When my mother caught James and me naked in our garage, she switched my bare behind—not the wisest response to a boy coping with the mysteries of sexuality. That punishment and a later, unrelated fiery sermon of a missionary priest scared the hell out of me and resulted in guilt feelings that hung over me for years. So I sometimes confessed to my mother, kneeling beside her bed in the morning before leaving for school and attending the mass that preceded it. She assured me that I wasn't going to hell for harboring impure thoughts, a Catholic Church identification of sexual inclination. Priests in confession, however, were less comforting. My making a fervent act of contrition as prescribed by the confessor in keeping with the rules of the Church, along with a penance of three "Our Fathers" and three "Hail Marys" led nowhere in assuaging my guilty feelings.

One of my journal entries describes a bus trip from Lawton to Oklahoma City to visit my grandparents and cousin in late August when I was about ten years old. My family called me Mickey until I announced at thirteen that my name was Mike.

Mickey had gotten on the bus just after school on Friday. His parents had left earlier, but he had to practice for a recital scheduled for the Wesley (Chapel United) Methodist Church in early October. He knew the bus route by heart, every turn, especially between Chickasha and Blanchard. The view from the window of the Trailways bus was an unending stretch of sandy, reddish soil, most of the grass brown and frightened-looking by now but hanging on. The sky was a clear, late-summer blue-gray, the sun bright, the air dry with a hint of coolness from the bus's noisy air conditioner which did little more than distract riders from the heat. Ten years old, of average height with glasses, a gap-toothed smile, and freckles, Mickey escaped looking clichéd because in Oklahoma, few kids looked like that. He sat, content, looking past the bus driver and up the narrow road, occasionally tuning in to the conversations between a man and woman across the aisle. They were arguing about how he knew she was going to spill the Dr. Pepper in her cup after she told the soda fountain lady to put more ice in.

Aunt Jeannette, who taught music at grand and spinet pianos in her living room, encouraged my interest in music. When my piano teacher, Mrs. Weller, proved to be very competent, I played classical pieces in recitals and had a college scholarship offered after a superior rating for my performance of a George Gershwin prelude. I never knew Mrs. Weller's first name.

Meanwhile, I read few books except for thin, well-illustrated volumes in geography after checking the number of pages before taking a book out of the library. Each month, I bought the only copy of *Theater Arts* at a local drugstore as well as *Song Hits* magazine and sheet music from Broadway plays to play and sing. I was thrilled to see the musical *High Button Shoes* when my aunt took me to see it in Oklahoma City, Later, although I never read plays by George Bernard Shaw, I was happy to see *Don Juan in Hell* with Charles Laughton, Charles Boyer, and Tyrone Power and *Candida* with Olivia de Havilland.

Movies (never "films" in those days) made my connection with the wider world. Although my southern Baptist friends couldn't go to movies on Sundays, I saw at least two a week. Five constituted the record for one week when the musical *Words and Music* about Richard Rodgers and Lorenz Hart showed at the Lawton Theater. A smaller theater made foreign films available, and I saw Charles Chaplin and Claire Bloom in *Limelight*. I also saw the Italian movies *Bicycle Thieves* and *Open City*, each unforgettable for different reasons.

During the Second World War, a wider world invaded Lawton, as two hundred thousand or more soldiers and their families descended upon our quiet hometown of eighteen thousand people. Many servicemen came to Fort Sill for basic artillery training shortly before going overseas. Our large two-story house had a basement (uncommon in that part of the country) where my older brother Bob and I slept during wartime. My mother, who couldn't turn away anyone who needed a place to live, rented the three upstairs bedrooms to young officers and their wives. She also rented the small house that my grandparents owned next door. The fact that our house was filled with people from throughout the United States provided in itself an ongoing geography lesson for me. At Christmas and on other holidays, our parents turned our house over to the guests while we traveled to Oklahoma City to visit my grandparents.

The center of my early years was St. Mary's School with many of the same classmates from kindergarten through high school. For teachers, we had Sisters of Divine Providence in full black and white habits from the mother house in San Antonio. They faithfully taught a somewhat scruffy group of able students, some of them so-called problem children sent to Catholic school to learn discipline. Tuition was three dollars a month or two if your family belonged to Blessed Sacrament parish, the only Catholic church in town. Some students paid nothing, since their families lived without most of the amenities we take for granted. Although my father probably never earned more than six thousand dollars a year or in the vicinity of fifty-five thousand dollars a year in 2019, people in the parish regarded our family as among the wealthier

Michael, left, with his parents,
Guy Herbert True and Agnes Murphy True
(green markings appear on original photo)

members, perhaps because we belonged to the local country club since my dad enthusiastically played golf.

The ten nuns staffing the school, their lives dedicated to the church and our education, lived in a two-story house next door. Sister Mary Ignatia, my favorite high school teacher, taught my favorite subject, math, and physics, chemistry, typing, Latin, and ancient history. She disapproved of my choosing basketball over advanced algebra. Intelligent and independent with a wry smile, she probably had a professional career before she entered the convent. She maintained her personal integrity even as she obeyed rules set down by the superior.

Most of the girls in my classes made their own clothes. Mary Krueger, an Oklahoma sister to Willa Cather's Antonia, designed and cut out dresses, hurriedly pinning a skirt in essential places to be ready for Easter Sunday and midnight mass at Christmas. Flora Landoll, one of the middle children in a family of twelve, and her younger sister Ruthie, whom I dated, lived on a farm two miles from school and managed to look beautiful in simple dresses made from flower sacks. Billie Margaret Outenreath was probably the brightest in our group. By the sixth grade, she read giant novels while I scored poorly on vocabulary quizzes and stumbled over words that she could spell, define, and give synonyms for. Her life was hard, however, since her family had little money and occasionally got singled out in the local newspaper for disorderly conduct, which must have embarrassed her. From sixth grade on, she had frequent kissing parties at her house. Blindfolded, we held out our hands with thumbs up so the boy or girl named "it" could choose someone to pair with.

Except for tennis, my athletic skills were limited. I never caught the football thrown to me over the goal line or connected the bat to the softball, something of an embarrassment to my older brother who coached the team. As captain of the high school basketball team, I scored one basket the whole season as the cheering section went wild. I got to pick up the trophy when our team won the division championship in Oklahoma City.

Thanks to the nuns, my high school background served me well academically. In high school, a drill-sergeant principal had destroyed whatever interest I had in poetry by making us memorize large chunks of Henry Wadsworth Longfellow ("By the shores of Gitchie Gumie,/By the shining big sea water . . .") as punishment for talking in class. Even she couldn't undermine the close friendships among my classmates, however, when she canceled our senior prom because several of us drank beer at a house party.

Father Ben Hulshof, pastor of the parish, was also superintendent of schools. A thoughtful, rather formal person educated at the University of

Louvain, Belgium, he was a kind confessor who listened to my list of venial, then mortal, sins, agonizingly admitted in the boxy confessional or in the sanctuary before 6 a.m. mass. From the fourth grade through high school, I served as an altar boy and later sang in the choir on special feast days and Christmas Eve. The high drama of Holy Week concluded with a five-hour ceremony on Holy Saturday—blessing the Easter fire, candle, and holy water and singing the Litany of the Saints. After the lengthy liturgy, altar boys and choir girls met for breakfast at a restaurant owned by our classmates' parents. The celebration marked the end of Lenten fast and abstinence and the beginning of the Easter Season.

My closest friends included Allen Ray Lehman and several other army brats who lived in military quarters at Fort Sill, and our experiences there extended into World War II. Staying there overnight, we occasionally heard artillery shells whizzing over the house and landing on practice ranges in the nearby Wichita Mountains. Living on the post, my friends enjoyed perks unavailable to us civilians unless they invited us to swim at the officers' or enlisted men's clubs (all men in those days) or to shop at the post exchange or PX. Their youth auxiliary sponsored frequent nifty dances at the polo club on hot summer nights when the air was dry and the moon was full. Most children of military families ended up in some branch of the service, so I rarely saw them after graduation from high school.

My close friend Leroy Shepler, the oldest child in a family with financial and mental hardships, was intelligent but rather obstreperous in school. His wise counsel regarding "occasions of sin" during adolescence made particular sense. He argued that, if one were destined for hell for committing one so-called impure act, the nunny circumlocution for masturbation, the penalty couldn't be any worse if one repeated the crime several times before his next confession.

Until I was about twelve, my closest friend was Jimmie France, the only child of my mother's closest friend, Iravene. Since they lived more than a mile away, I often schemed to extend my visits to his home by hiding behind the garage door so that my mother couldn't find me. Never a dull moment with Jimmie. A favorite game involved hiding from cars in the huge sewer pipes at a construction site near my home while quizzing one another on state capitals and names of rivers around the world. Intelligent, Jimmie also was a good athlete, but I managed to stump him when he mistakenly named Decatur rather than Springfield as the capital of Illinois or confused Hartford, Connecticut, with Lexington, Kentucky.

We both enjoyed following college football and attended the annual invitational basketball tournament at Christmastime in Oklahoma City. When our parents went out for the evening, we stayed at his grandmother's house next door. We listened to basketball games on a small, dimly lit radio before falling asleep in his uncle's double bed. The popular sportscaster Curt Gowdy announced Oklahoma A & M basketball games, including the heartbreaking final when Holy Cross College of Worcester, Massachusetts, beat A and M for the 1947 National Collegiate Athletic Association championship. A special pleasure of spending the night at the France home was the breakfast his mother fixed for us the next morning: bacon, scrambled eggs, toast, and all the trimmings. Years later and far from home, I kept trying to recover the aroma and taste of that exotic meal.

Jimmie was the first person beyond my family whom I loved, and my feelings for him remain strong, though he lives far away and seldom responds to telephone messages or birthday greetings. When I see a young person who resembles him with light, olive-colored skin with high coloring in his cheeks and dark hair, I instinctively turn and look again.

Although I was not aware of it at the time, the vivid, witty speech that characterized conversations between my mother and her friends set a standard by which I still judge language. None of them tolerated pretense or foolishness nor were they intimidated by anyone considered important. Was their colorful, imagistic speech related to their not having spent too much time in school? Tagging along with my mother at the wheel, driving around town sometimes talking and sometimes not, I was never bored in her company. Inevitably, she had projects to complete—a slipcover to make or a meal to prepare with special ingredients available only at Gartrell's Grocery

Michael, right, with friends, about 1950

Store. Whatever the project, it had to be done now.

When I was thirteen, the France family took me with them on a trip to southern California to attend the annual Junior Rose Bowl game in Pasadena. My brother Bob was on the football team of the local junior college playing in the game, and also because I had never been outside of Oklahoma and Texas, I could hardly believe my good fortune. We drove southwest of Lawton across west Texas to Lubbock and then Roswell, New Mexico, through the Alamogordo proving grounds. We spent the first night in Las Cruces and the second in Tucson. After a brief stop in Yuma, we spent the night with my grandmother's sister Jane in El Centro, California, where flowering poinsettias in her front yard amazed us. My brother's team lost the football game, unfortunately, but that event paled before my memories of San Juan Capistrano, Hollywood and Vine, the Los Angeles freeway, and the stunning and varied beauty of New Mexico's mountains and Arizona's deserts.

My brothers, seven and ten years older than I, were not central to my early life. They had left home by the time I was seven. Herb worked at Zale's Jewelry Store in Oklahoma City, served briefly in the marines, and then enrolled at the University of Oklahoma. Two months after his seventeenth birthday, Bob enlisted in the navy in 1944 near the end of World War II. During their late adolescent escapades, however, I was privy to my parents' sleepless nights and vigils at the upstairs window awaiting their return from parties or travels to distant places. I remember crying through midnight mass on Christmas Eve 1944, as my parents worried as the aircraft carrier Bob was assigned to conducted missions between Bremerton, Washington, and the South Pacific.

After my brothers left home, I spent much time with my parents, so my place in the family was favored, shared with my dog Tuffy. School work, practicing piano, and odd jobs babysitting, working at a laundry or golf driving range, delivering stationery at an office supply store, and sweeping floors at J. C. Penney occupied most of my time. Years later, as an admirer of the novels and essays of Gore Vidal, I realized that my street was named for his grandfather, the blind Senator Thomas Pryor Gore from Oklahoma, and that his mother had been born in Lawton.

When I graduated from high school, my parents expected me to attend Cameron Junior College in Lawton, like my brother Bob, but I insisted on going directly to the University of Oklahoma in Norman, which held a certain magic for me ever since I had visited Herb there years before. As a freshman, I roomed with someone I knew, Clarence Henry Gold, a graduate of the big public high school in Lawton. I soon adapted to the atmosphere of the big state university with ten thousand students. Since tuition was only sixty-six dollars a semester for state residents with room and board at about a hundred dollars a month, I could earn most of the money for my expenses through summer jobs at the local Oldsmobile dealer or cleaning helicopters at a Fort Sill hangar. Fortunately, my parents covered remaining expenses.

During the first fall semester, I made the pilgrimage to the Cotton Bowl in Dallas for the annual Oklahoma-Texas football game during the Texas State Fair. At a pep rally the night before the game, I screamed my lungs out on the street between the Baker and Adolphus hotels in downtown Dallas. I also got dutifully drunk on whiskey sours, a traditional rite of passage for anyone growing up in Oklahoma, then still dry. The next morning, I attended mass with a terrible hangover before the two-hundred-mile trip back to Norman.

Regarded as a good student in my small high school, I soon learned that some OU classmates were smarter than I and resigned myself to a scaled-down academic performance. Horsing around the dorm, playing piano in the common room late at night, and gossiping about campus life, fraternities, and sororities left little time for study. I was lucky to complete the first year with a B average. Clearing tables in the dining hall for fifty cents an hour required my signing a statement saying that I was not nor never had been a member of the Communist Party. Never having planned to overthrow the American government, I should perhaps be grateful to the federal government for putting the idea into my head. The second semester, staffing the circulation desk at the university library paid a little better and acquainted me with books of literary criticism I hadn't known existed.

Although freshman year was mostly a lark, my love of literature, especially poetry, became apparent in a course with Paul Ruggiers, a Chaucer scholar and excellent teacher who introduced me to John Donne's sonnet, "Batter My Heart Three-Person's God," William Wordsworth's "Ode: Intimations of Immortality," Matthew Arnold's "Dover Beach," and T. S. Eliot's "The Love Song of J. Alfred Prufrock." As an undergraduate, I remained a curious but casual student, arriving late for Shakespeare class and then falling asleep as I assumed the teacher was unaware of what I was up to. In my second year, I moved into the Delta Tau Delta fraternity house, where my roommate's Stromberg-Carlson radio boomed the 1950s hit "Rock around the Clock" across the campus.

The prescribed curriculum meant taking courses in Latin and Greek literature in translation, for which I remain grateful, although my focus was on American literature with a minor in French. By my junior year, I still had no plans for after graduation and spent most of my time on everything but study. My grades bottomed out, making it easier for me to win a small grant for grade improvement during senior year. The check arrived soon after I began graduate study the following semester.

Student deferments kept many of us in college during the Korean War, while high school friends went off to East Asia. Two of my high school classmates died in plane crashes. Twenty-two OU classmates, including fraternity brothers, died in a plane crash as they returned home after naval ROTC summer camp in 1952. In spite of such sobering experiences, no one that I knew ever questioned that war or the emerging American

23

empire accompanying it. Nor did anyone in my acquaintance, including professors, indicate precise knowledge of Korea. Only years later when I prepared to travel to Pyongyang, North Korea, to lecture on nonviolence at the Juche Institute did I learn about atrocities of the Korean war, including American and British planes bombing and then burning everything in their path after retreating from the Yalu River.

Although fraternities were all the rage on campus, I had little interest in them initially. After a month or so, however, I knew names and ranking of the Greek pecking order and was flattered to be invited to pledge Delta Tau Delta at the end of my freshman year. That was probably a mistake, since popular and cool business majors from Oklahoma City and Tulsa set the standard for that culture. Although I remained skeptical about the flashing lights and mumbo-jumbo associated with fraternity initiation, I worked at being accepted rather unsuccessfully except for several lasting friendships. I remember few political discussions over three years among my fraternity brothers. Although they made frequent jokes about one another being gay, accusations of homosexuality provoked fierce reactions. A handsome pledge was thrown out of the house—and perhaps the university—after being accused of homosexual involvement with a football player at Jeff House, the dorm for athletes.

A redeeming social value of fraternity life was a chorus directed by an annual senior member. It habitually won the annual all-university sing. My successive roommates included the son of an army sergeant who, after studying medicine at Columbia, remained in military service; a hotshot graduate of Oklahoma City's Central High School who completed a residency in ophthalmology at Johns Hopkins before chairing that department at the University of Oklahoma Medical School; a marketing major and later Republican who practices law in upstate New York; an electrical engineer who went on to a successful career in the oil business. Another roommate, a son of wealthy parents, read the daily *Wall Street Journal,* played the stock market, and kept a pistol strapped to his bedpost. Coming home late from working at the library and entering our bedroom, I sometimes feared that he might blow my brains out if he failed to identify me.

The political atmosphere at OU in the early 1950s was appropriately Eisenhowerish—that is, middle-of-the-road, although I had been warned by a restaurant owner in Lawton to watch out for Communists. The "Communists" turned out to be a professor of economics who refused to sign the unconstitutional loyalty oath required of state employees. Two of my favorite English professors were named radicals on a list published by the American Legion. My fraternity brother Dick Patten initiated a lively liberal journal, an effort to revive populism and rooted in the state's early history. Dick later studied economics at the University of Wisconsin and Harvard before working to initiate cooperative banks in Indonesia, where he was a colleague of President Barack Obama's mother.

Like two other Catholics in a fraternity of a hundred undergraduates, I got called a mackerel snapper. My religious identity was a topic of conversation on Fridays, when I didn't eat meat. An active member and later vice-president of the Newman Center, the campus Catholic student organization, I faithfully attended Sunday mass and daily mass during Lent. There was a particular feeling of belonging when I saw my favorite English teacher and head of the classics department at St. Thomas More Chapel. Eventually, my brothers and I endowed a Newman Center lecture series named for our parents. Since then, my grandnephew Sam Gonzales graduated from OU, the tenth member of my family to do so since 1915.

Fraternity and sorority parties and sports dominated the social life of the campus, and the university football team dominated the NCAA national rankings during the 1950s. My social life was limited to occasional dates for fraternity dances. Scholars and teachers made it possible for me to learn a great deal, and the library's collection and the university press qualified as first rate. Although I failed to take full advantage of that culture, I received the beginning of an education almost in spite of myself. After initial success as a math major, I gradually lost interest in courses geared toward petroleum engineers and changed my major to English with later regrets that I wasn't alert enough at the time to pursue a double major in mathematics and literature.

Exceptionally good teachers—Stanley Coffman, Jewel Wurtzbaugh, and Victor Elconin—enabled me to move through the English program with requirements in various literatures. A special bonus during my last semester was a course in the history of science after Professor Wayne Rollins joined the faculty and oversaw the famous DeGolyer Collection in geology. In time, I fell in love with the idea of a university long before I read John Henry Newman's treatise on the topic. Especially memorable courses include "Critical Theories of the Eighteenth Century" with John Raines's stunning lectures on Jean-Antoine Watteau's painting, "The Embarkation for Cythera," exhilarating performances of Mozart sonatas, and readings of Alexander Pope's long satirical poem, "The Rape of the Lock." In courses on Renaissance literature, Dr. Wurtzbaugh, eccentric but formidable scholar who admired Edmund Spenser's long poem "The Faerie Queen," gave moving commentary on Donne's sermons and George Herbert's religious lyrics.

I was drawn to university life not out of love of scholarship but out of interest in the architecture and beautiful OU campus: sturdy, handsome buildings in understated Cherokee Gothic, walkways, elm trees, and flower beds of tiger lilies during sensual warm days at the beginning of the fall semester. I also loved spring evenings under the wide sky—the Milky Way and North Star seemingly just beyond reach. Walking across campus after class on my way to the student union for coffee always struck me as glamorous.

Returning from vacation and driving across the bridge over the South Canadian River near the campus, I was aware of my heart beating faster and feeling excitement and anticipation. The same thing happened when I returned for the fiftieth anniversary of my OU graduation. At that time, John Havenstrite, my former roommate, and I found that the university was going through a renaissance with new museums of fine arts and natural history. David Boren, a former Rhodes Scholar and US Senator, served as president. Although Oklahoma had long been one of the poorer states, it traditionally ranked among the top ten states in proportion of wealth devoted to public education, from which I benefited. Large private universities that I visited over the years, including Duke where I studied, struck me as rather hot-housie or pretentious in their Gothic trapping. The OU campus, by contrast, strikes me as authentic, just about right. The same was true of my former classmates when we became reacquainted at reunion festivities.

As an undergraduate, I obviously spent too many hours at the bridge table, where a game began just after supper and often continued until two or four in the morning. Finally, during my senior year, I chose studying over fraternity or campus distraction. Everyone told us that we were The Silent Generation, whatever that meant. However they respond to the times, students never live up to people's depictions of them. In our case, the faculty was pleasantly surprised when the campus rowdies initiated a panty raid in the spring of my sophomore year. Sorority members dangled pink underthings from second-floor windows as young men obliged them by raiding their bedrooms and collecting dainty trophies before moving on to the next residence. The only casualties were students caught aiming canisters of tear gas at campus police when the crowd got a bit out of hand. Years later, when I mentioned that bit of fifties activism to undergraduate students I taught, they looked at me as if I were a ridiculous as well as dirty old man. Little did they know how radically their social lives, with men and women living in the same dorms, differed from my own in college. Although I had women friends on campus and dates for fraternity parties and dances, there were no serious romances. A rather predictable, expected relationship with a member of Tri-Delt sorority ended shortly after graduation. That part of my life changed significantly for the better after I moved to Minneapolis.

Against all inclination but on the advice of a friend, I opted to remain in the Reserve Officers' Training Corps, or ROTC, program beyond the two years required at a land-grant institution and thus had the prospect of graduating as an officer in the army. Perhaps already a pacifist without

Michael in Army ROTC, about 1951

knowing it, since I'd never met one, I gave a rousing speech in ROTC classes that took the army's side against Senator Joseph McCarthy of Wisconsin shortly before he ran afoul of Congress.

When I attended summer camp at Fort Benning, Georgia, at the end of my junior year, I managed to flunk out of ROTC. Training sessions involving rifle practice on the firing line, crawling under simulated gunfire, and negotiating my way through a minefield seemed unreal to me. At the driving range, Abbott Nelson and I spent hours pulling targets in the rifle pit. Failing to score high enough to qualify, we eventually cheated our way to completing that part of basic training. Sweaty and dirty throughout the long afternoon, we heard bullets bite the dust several feet below the target. Turning toward one another and announcing "Another bullseye!" as we collapsed with laughter, we pulled the target, punched a black marker at the center of it, and ran it back up.

The summer was something of a fiasco except for a weekend with four classmates in the New Orleans French Quarter. We stayed at bargain prices in a room that hummed all night long over the rotating hotel bar at the Hotel Monteleon. We enjoyed dinner at Antoine's, singing at Pat O'Brien's, and dinner at the Famous Door where the band paraded on top of the bar while playing "The Saints Go Marchin' In."

At the beginning of the fall semester, the university's ROTC commander called me in to give me the sad news that I had failed summer camp. When I told my adviser, Professor Wurtzbaugh, she almost fell out of her chair laughing. To my great joy, escaping ROTC my senior year enabled me to spend Tuesday afternoons playing bridge instead of attending weekly drills or sleeping through impossibly boring military science courses.

A Hillel Foundation singalong with a guitar-playing student named Bob Simha introduced many of us to the songs of Woody Guthrie, who later became a central figure on the literature of the 1930s. Dick Patten drove several of us to Oklahoma City for a rally supporting Adlai Stevenson. My teachers' political sympathies, from liberal to populist, were more interesting than those of conservative academics with whom I taught later. Over a forty-year period, my colleagues at various universities seldom raised a cry against Holy Mother, the State, as the US came to dominate the world militarily and economically, while rich nations pocketed the world's wealth at the expense of the poor, and as the nuclear clock moved closer to midnight.

Accepted for graduate study at the University of Wisconsin, Madison, where two favored professors had completed doctorates, and at the University of Minnesota, I decided to check out the latter following my graduation from OU. While visiting the Twin Cities in July of 1959, I landed a job as a counselor with the office of the dean of students, which enabled me to pay in-state tuition of $125 a quarter. As the home state of my grandparents and birthplace of my father, aunts, and uncles, Minnesota and the culture of the upper Midwest had certain resonance for me from the moment I arrived.

Although my older brothers and I had moved away, Lawton—which had grown into a rather disjointed, sprawling city of a hundred thousand people—remained my parents' home. My brothers and our extended family gathered there periodically, especially when my parents celebrated their fiftieth wedding anniversary in 1969. My father died in 1980 shortly after their sixtieth wedding anniversary and my mother, six years later, to be buried in a plot in a wide stretch of land between the city and the army base. Their resting place resembles the burial ground in Willa Cather's short story "Neighbor Risky," where

> the grass grew over the graves and hid the fence; the few evergreens stood out black in it, shadows in a pool. The sky was very blue and soft, the stars rather faint because the moon was full.

With my parents and brothers gone, Oklahoma seems very far away though vivid in memory.

Minnesota, North Carolina, Indiana, 1955

I'd just as soon be pushed by events to where I belong.
—William Stafford

Having previously visited the university and the city, I arrived at the Rock Island railroad station in Minneapolis in September 1955 with positive expectations. While serving as a resident counselor at the Delt House, I soon discovered that the Newman Center, two doors away, was something of a nerve center on campus. Its cafeteria, bookstore, drama group, non-credit seminars, engaging liturgical services, and literary magazine made it a lively meeting place. Visiting artists and scholars included J. F. Powers, John LaFarge, SJ; W. H. Auden, John Courtney Murray, SJ; Flannery O'Connor, John Cogley, and John Charlot as well as Allen Tate and John Berryman, university faculty who frequented the center.

Father George Garrelts, director of the campus Newman Center and well-known and in great demand in the Twin Cities, was responsible for much of the activity, having been recently named a promising young professional by Time Magazine. A native of Illinois and diocesan priest educated at the seminaries of St. Louis and St. Paul, he admired John Henry Newman, the great nineteenth century Oxford scholar, priest, and literary personality recognized by many as the spiritual father of Vatican II. George's range of interests and friendships as well as his genuine connection to students and remarkable talent for liturgy contributed to his success as a chaplain. Before Vatican II, he implemented liturgical changes with a religious perspective that influenced American Catholicism through the 1980s. I made an effort to get to know him, sometimes taking long walks with him in the evening, the one time of day when I knew I had his full attention.

Although he wrote several books, he was much better known for other talents, including an ability to capture in a single phrase the essence of a literary work, film, or lecture. His imagination and originality led to his later success when, in a parish, he became the refuge of educated and ordinary Catholics throughout the region. Banished from the Newman Center and appointed pastor of St. Frances Cabrini Catholic Church in Minneapolis, he attracted many new parishioners and visitors. His popularity inevitably led to the hierarchy's regarding him with suspicion. After taking a leave to complete a doctorate at Syracuse University, he left the priesthood and married. The move was a common story among other talented priests as the institutional church moved away from the promise of Vatican II. Afterward, George made the most of his gifts as a chaplain at Rensselaer Polytechnic Institute in Troy, New York, and professor at Mercyhurst College in Erie, Pennsylvania. I learned much from George about religion, literature, and how to conduct myself as a teacher and community organizer beyond the classroom. Our friendship over fifty years is one of the gifts of my life.

Graduate students in English whom I met at the Newman Center became my closest associates, lively men and women who combined love of literature and partying in equal measure. The father of one of them managed a country club in South St. Paul. The mother of another (legend had it that she had danced with F. Scott Fitzgerald at the White Bear Yacht Club) hosted events at her mansion with a dance floor and bandstand in the basement. Our purported reason for meeting in her library—with a great sculptured ceiling and well-framed view of downtown Minneapolis—was to study for the master-of-arts exam. At each study session, scotch flowed freely throughout the evening. Shortly before midnight, we moved to the large, handsome dining room where the hostess served coffee in china cups and silver service.

My modest campus digs across the tracks from Dinky Town prompted me to spend little time there.

Over the next two years, although I seldom let my studies toward the MA degree interfere with my social life, I managed to learn a lot along the way. The faculty in the English department was one of the strongest in the country, and although I knew little about them beforehand, I soon realized that I was studying among truly remarkable artists, teachers, scholars, and students with strong undergraduate backgrounds. They included Sumner Ferris, a brilliant Harvard alumnus, and former students of Austin Warren, a well-known literary critic at the University of Michigan. Although my study habits had improved little since my undergraduate days, my formal education proceeded nonetheless because of my teachers and associates and the intellectual environment we all inhabited.

Allen Tate, poet and critic, was responsible for my growing appreciation of modern poetry. His courses, lectures, and readings included casual references to his friendship with major writers of the period, including Eliot and John Crowe Ransom. Simply by reading it aloud, Tate conveyed a strong sense of a poem's distinctive character and power. That was particularly true of Emily Dickinson's lyric poems and Eliot's *The Waste Land*, as well as the stories of Flannery O'Connor, Tate's friend then in her early thirties. His wife, the novelist Caroline Gordon, had edited O'Connor's early work, then widely read at colleges and universities in the upper Midwest.

Smoking a cigarette in the classroom, Tate sat behind a desk on a platform in front of the room. Sometimes he read from his own essays or made pertinent comments about an image or line of a poem. His voice with its soft, elegant southern accent conveyed the spirit as well as, without intruding on it, the meaning of a poem with an acute sense of its sound and rhythm. For his writing seminar, I managed to write a short story based upon an incident in my great-grandmother's life, a version of it later published in *Ms.* magazine. For the seminar, I also wrote an essay on Dickinson published in the *Newman Annual*.

While still an undergrad at Vanderbilt University in Nashville, Tate was one of the first people fully to appreciate Eliot's *The Waste Land*. He and Eliot, born in Missouri and expatriated to England, remained friends for years. At the end of my second year at Minnesota, Eliot arrived on campus to read his famous essay, "Frontiers of Criticism at the Present

Time," before an audience of sixteen thousand in the university's sports palace. Minneapolis qualified as perhaps the only city in the world that could attract such a large, appreciative audience for such a topic and presenter. In an eloquent introduction, Tate acknowledged his debt to Eliot and repeated the latter's dedication of *The Waste Land* to the poet Ezra Pound: "a il miglior fabbro"—"to the better maker."

Besides Tate's courses, I studied seventeenth- and eighteenth-century English literature with Samuel Hope Monk, a brilliant scholar and teacher and Tate's longtime friend and office mate. Knowing almost nothing about the Augustan age, I eventually enrolled in almost every course Monk offered. Like Tate and, in different ways, William Van O'Connor and Huntington Brown, Monk set a high standard that contributed to the rich campus literary culture.

Near the end of my first year at a seminar on Gerard Manley Hopkins at the Newman Center, I met Mary Pat Delaney, a friend of several women in my graduate classes. Shortly afterward, we attended a costume party at the fraternity house and spoke several times on the phone. When I invited her to accompany me to the Eliot lecture, however, she turned me down. If she had had a bad time on the first date, she added, she would have accepted. Since she had a good time and because she had plans to enter the Convent of the Sisters of the Visitation in a month, she had to say no.

Nine months later, at the first word of her leaving the convent, I phoned her for a date, and we were out dancing at the St. Paul Hotel the following weekend. During the winter, I rode the University Avenue bus to St. Paul, then walked a mile in the bitter cold to her family home on Portland Avenue. Fortunately for me, she agreed to type the three research papers required for the MA degree. A year later, after my time in the army, we were married in St. Luke's Church, just a block from her home.

Although I was interested in politics, my education regarding public issues developed slowly as the rich history of Minnesota, home to the Farmer Labor Party and other progressive movements, insinuated its way into my political consciousness. After high school friends died in plane crashes during the Korean War, I became aware of the consequences of US military and foreign policy and dangers posed by weapons of mass destruction. I signed my name on a petition circulated in the Minnesota English department, just below Allen Tate's signature, that called for an end to nuclear testing. As the civil rights movement unfolded, I met people familiar with the Catholic Worker movement and began reading its newspaper. A lecture by Henry Steele Commager strengthened my liberal sympathies, but it was some time before I became aware of my populist roots as an Okie or committed myself to political issues or candidates.

In my second year at Minnesota, I received a teaching fellowship, mainly grading papers, a task I performed with little competence, I fear. Still, the experience of working with younger members of the department, like Fred Higginson, gave me a clearer sense of what teaching might be like and confirmed me in my plans to pursue a doctorate at some point.

Soon after completing a master's degree in May 1957, I left for six months in the army to fulfill my military obligations. As a result of a casual conversation with someone knowledgeable about the draft laws, I applied for and received a critical skills classification because of my plans to be a teacher. The classification required my spending only six months rather than two years on active duty and seven and a half years in the inactive reserve. Stationed at Fort Chaffee, Arkansas, near Fort Smith, I went through basic training once again, then spent several months as a clerk-typist on frequent duty with the kitchen police among pots and pans, dutifully defending my country. Lying on their bunks in the barracks, my fellow recruits read Grace Metalious's *Peyton Place* while I pored over Allen Ginsberg's recently published *Howl*. Off duty, I frequented the post library and a beer bar in Fort Smith, the Squeeze Inn.

On completion of my army assignment, I returned to Minneapolis in the midst of an economic recession. Having a hard time finding a job of any kind, I shared a grubby apartment on the west bank of the Mississippi River with my friend Marvin Dodge. For two months, almost until the time of our wedding on April 12, 1958, I spent days pounding the pavement, having interviews, and taking tests for everything from carrying mail to selling insurance. Evenings I spent looking over shower gifts from Mary Pat's many friends and helping her select patterns for china and silverware. Her cousin actually hosted a so-called shower for me.

Three weeks before our wedding, I finally landed a job as a technical writer for Remington-Rand UNIVAC. At the

*Michael and Mary Pat Delaney
on their wedding day, April 12, 1958*

time, I had no qualms about working for a defense contractor. I spent most of my time either loafing on the job or writing positive accounts of its computer-guided missile systems. My experiences there made me aware of America's military-industrial-university-ecclesiastical complex and the brainwashing and battle babble that perpetuate it.

After our wedding, my wife and I settled in St. Paul, where both of us worked full time as editors while I applied for further graduate study. Eventually, I chose Duke because of its well-known program in American literature and rumors of financial support for needy students. Soon, we expected our first child, due nine months and two weeks after our wedding. Shortly after our daughter's birth in January 1959, I flew to Durham, North Carolina, to begin classes. Mary Pat and Mary Laurel followed three weeks later.

* * *

My first day in Durham contrasted sharply with my first day in Minneapolis four days earlier. In spite of my familiarity with the Southwest, I was surprised how the peculiarities of the real South affected me. The smell of tobacco permeated the air in Durham during a persistently rainy season while native southerners and the general culture felt less welcoming than the culture of where I had previously lived. Apartments were either expensive or hard to find, and the formal atmosphere of the university differed from the relative informality of the U of M.

The first apartment we took in a working-class area of town belonged to a southern Baptist family native to Durham. Everything went well in the interview until I answered the question of the woman who owned the apartment with her husband about my religion. When I said I was a Catholic, the rocking chair she sat in came to an abrupt standstill. "I don't think this will work out at all," she said. During continuing conversation, I apparently relieved her fears about my religious affiliation. Then I moved into a rather rundown, three-room apartment on the first floor of their rental property. My first night there, before Mary Pat and Mary Laurel joined me, left me worried about whether the apartment would adequately serve our new family far away from home. Fortunately, they felt less hesitant about the place than I, and we soon made friends with an Iraqi couple and their daughter who lived across the hall.

Duke's English department, including a number of graduate students, was smaller and less varied than Minnesota's. The faculty seemed rather aloof or at least distant in their relationships with students. Beginning classes and preparing for the German exam, I hitchhiked or took a bus over a mile to campus and spent most of my days at my carrel in the university library. We had enough money to make it through the first semester with tuition at a thousand dollars a semester. Until I received a teaching fellowship the following year, I took a part-time job as a ward secretary at Duke University Hospital. Mary Pat worked as a secretary in the psychology department before and after the birth of our second child.

In the meantime, we hired Sarah Boykin, an African-American woman, to take care of our daughter and to share half of Mary Pat's salary, which was $250 a month. Sarah, who lived in a small house without running water three blocks without sidewalks from us took an early liking to our daughter. Telling us about wheeling Mary Laurel downtown in a stroller, Sarah spoke proudly about how white folks stopped their cars and waited for her to cross the street, because they knew on sight that Mary Laurel was "a rich folks' baby." We never knew Sarah's age exactly, but when she told us about losing a son in the flu epidemic of 1918 "because he was too smart for a black folks' baby," we assumed she was in her late sixties. After Michael's birth at the university hospital in April 1960, Sarah was equally solicitous of him.

During my first Duke summer session, I met Charles Fenton, a vital and productive young scholar of American literature. He had reputation for kindness and genuine interest in students. The youngest member of the department, he had published a much-admired book on Ernest Hemingway's apprenticeship. Handsome, witty with a bit of swagger, and former member of the Yale faculty, he had joined the Duke faculty at forty as a full professor, practically unheard of at the time.

A truly remarkable teacher, Fenton was particularly effective in conveying the significance of a literary work and its social, political, and historical background with just enough gossipy commentary to bring its author to life. Soon, he was immensely popular, and over the next year and a half, I enrolled in as many of his courses as possible. I audited several others. Often when I arrived at my library carrel in the morning, books and articles awaited me on topics we had discussed the previous day, and I looked forward to the possibility of his directing my dissertation.

Through Sarah Boykin and several incidents with our white neighbors, we learned a lot about indignities endured by people of color who lived nearby. By early 1960, four black college students in Greensboro eighty miles away sat down at a segregated lunch counter in Woolworth's and brought the civil rights movement home to us. I knew nothing at the time about founding of the Student Nonviolent Coordinating Committee in Raleigh in 1960 nor the first conference of Students for Democratic Society in Ann Arbor in 1959. The latter group often gathered in the living room of Elise and Kenneth Boulding, whom I met and with whom I worked closely years later. After the arrest of a chaplain at Yale, the brother of a classmate, on a freedom ride in Alabama, I began to pay closer attention to escalating turmoil, including arrests of civil rights activists and students throughout the South.

Although the undergraduate college at Duke remained segregated, the graduate school had integrated several years earlier. In 1960, graduate students passed out leaflets on campus asking people to join picket lines at local theaters where African Americans were relegated to the balcony. They called it "the crow's nest," a reference to Jim Crow laws condemning African Americans to second-class citizenship in the separate-but-equal atmosphere since the post-Civil-Wa erar. Eventually, I joined the picket line. I was certain a lone sniper in a tall building overlooking the street had his rifle aimed at me.

Local student leaders had participated in a sit-in in a drug store, thus indicating their skill, patience, discipline, and intelligence under duress. As we picketed a movie theater in Durham, they told all of us on the street to keep moving so as not to be arrested for blocking the right of way of people entering the building. They stationed observers at key sites along the picket line and at the end of the block to witness any confrontation or provocation by citizens or police. They cautioned us not to respond to hecklers or provocations verbal or other. It felt stunning to see young people scarcely twenty years old, already well-trained Gandhians, remaining cool and thoughtful, yet assertive. Police surrounded them as passersby eyed them suspiciously and a whole city waited for one false move to justify descending on them. Little did I realize at the time that the experience would lead to my involvement in social movements against nuclear weapons, US wars in Vietnam and Iraq, and teaching and scholarship on the history of nonviolence.

In the spring of 1961 when we ran out of money, I accepted a position teaching composition and introduction to literature at North Carolina College, an all-black college on the south side of Durham. Hospitable students and colleagues welcomed me as one of the few white faculty at the time, and Mary Pat and I had our first experience of being the only white couple at a large social gathering. Occasionally, older faculty members seemed to be part of the problem, as Stokely Carmichael said, rather than the solution. Like faculty elsewhere, they spoke condescendingly of their students and failed to recognize what some of them had accomplished in resisting discriminatory laws and practices in the community. For various reasons, I regarded my appointment as a gift and would have remained at the college if my family and I had not looked forward to returning to the Midwest.

The previous year, a graduate fellowship enabled me to teach at Duke, but even then, I lived under a cloud of grief and loss. On an early morning prior to the beginning of the fall semester, Charles Fenton committed suicide by jumping from the twelfth story of the Jack Tarr Durham Hotel. Reading about in the morning newspaper, I felt numb for several days with no feeling in my hands. The university did nothing to ease the pain for my fellow students, one of whom had been romantically involved with Fenton, nor for me. The funeral was a perfunctory affair before the body was shipped to Connecticut for burial. It was twenty years before I could speak about Fenton's death to anyone other than my wife. Although fifty years later I remain deeply grateful for him, I became aware that my grief included anger toward him for abandoning me in the middle of my program. Not an admirable reaction on my part but there nonetheless.

Fenton had been the subject of a novel *Fish Flying through Air* about his dropping out of college as an undergraduate, then enlisting in the Canadian Air Force during World War II. After his plane was shot down over the English Channel, he returned to Canada and the US to complete his undergraduate degree at Yale, marry, work as a journalist, and eventually complete a doctorate in American studies.

Three months after Fenton's death, I failed my preliminary exam, a two-hour ordeal before five senior faculty members. Although I had prepared for it, the occasion called for skills I had never learned. Disappointed—indeed, humiliated—I decided that the best antidote was to leave the university temporarily as soon as possible. Ironically, one professor who failed me on the examination recommended me for a teaching position in the Midwest, but when the chair of the English department at North Carolina College showed an interest in me, I seized the opportunity to remain in Durham, and I continued to teach there for a semester. Although all went on hold for a while, I continued my academic pursuits at Duke, where I eventually completed the doctorate. At Christmas, my family and I took a long train ride across the mid Southern states and the Appalachian Mountains to Oklahoma to visit my parents. Then we returned to Durham to teach. By happy accident, someone plowed into our hundred-dollar used car parked across the street from our home. The insurance enabled us to purchase an upscale two-hundred-dollar replacement.

In April, determined not to take a job that paid less than six thousand dollars a year, I accepted a position as assistant professor of English at Indiana State University, Terre Haute. With promises of a decent salary and permanent home, Mary Pat, Mary Laurel, Michael, and I left Durham for the Twin Cities, where I worked as a garbage man for the summer at a well-known restaurant. In late August, we moved to Terre Haute.

* * *

At Indiana State University, I taught courses in composition, introduction to literature, and soon, survey of American literature. My several colleagues were hospitable and congenial, especially the chair of the English department, George Smock. Students were eminently teachable. Whatever my limitations as a young teacher, I was fairly confident of my ability and immensely enjoyed all aspects of my work. Several of my well-educated and talented co-workers became close friends. Widely published Jim Light, for example, had a reputation that eventually led to his appointment as a major administrator at the City University of New York. I received invitations to lecture at the nearby St. Mary of the Woods College and Rose Polytechnic Institute, leading me to give occasional papers at regional professional associations. A virtue of our residence in Indiana was the opportunity to visit my brother Herb; his wife, Betty Ann, and their eight children in South Bend. Herb, who taught at Notre Dame before and after a successful career as a motivational speaker, remained an important influence in my life until his death in 2009.

My four years of teaching at Indiana State, with its excellent library, contributed substantially to my own education, and I read widely while preparing for classes and a second preliminary exam at Duke. After completing it, I spent part of a summer doing research at the Seth Low Library, Columbia University, among essential papers relating to my dissertation. Fortunately, Arlin Turner, a distinguished Nathaniel Hawthorne scholar as well as a thoughtful and helpful adviser at Duke, agreed to oversee my program after Fenton's death. Writing a dissertation turned out to be the high point of my formal education. Although I had previously limited scholarship to class assignments, I began for the first time to think of myself as a writer. I greatly benefited from Mary Pat's talent and generosity as an editor.

My dissertation topic, an ideal choice for me, was the American social and literature critic Randolph Bourne(1886-1918), who was deeply involved in literary and social movements during the period of early Modernism. Bourne's role as a socialist in educational reform and in the arts led me to regard the years between 1909 and 1918 as perhaps the richest in American history. The political atmosphere reflected the strength of the labor movement, populist, progressive, and other movements when Eugene Victor Debs's newspaper, *Appeal to Reason*, had 750,000 subscribers. Between about 1908 and 1921, the United States was a hotbed of political and aesthetic initiatives, including the 1913 Armory Show, also known as the International Exhibition of Modern Art, and founding of the National Association for the Advancement of Colored People, American Friends Service Committee, Fellowship of Reconciliation, Women's International League for Peace and Freedom, *Poetry Magazine,* and *The New Republic.* One of Bourne's essays appeared in the first issue of Schofield Thayer's *Dial* magazine, where poems of Pound, William Butler Yeats, Eliot, e. e. cummings, and William Carlos Williams first appeared.

Personal relationships among socialists and anarchists, writers and radicals including Eugene O'Neill, Dorothy Day, Emma Goldman, Theodore Dreiser, Alfred Stieglitz, and Amy Lowell contributed to an artistic and political renaissance. Bourne associated with many of them and wrote an important book on the Gary Schools and film, literature, and social theory. Challenging John Dewey's support of US entrance on the side of the allies in World War I, Bourne became regarded as a kind of patron saint of the literary culture that emerged after his death in 1918. In "War and the Intellectuals" and similar essays, he anticipated the spirit of individual intellectuals, including Ernest Hemingway, who referred to World War I as "that senseless slaughter." "History of a Literary Radical," title essay of his posthumous collection, would inform the work of the lost generation as did the antiwar poems of Wilfred Owen, Ezra Pound, and Robert Graves.

By the mid to late sixties, I became somewhat knowledgeable about contemporary poetry, including that of the Beats. I invited Brother Antoninus, née William Everson, to read at Indiana State. His poetry as well as his manner of presentation in full Dominican habit gave his presentations and conversation a dramatic air. In spite of his occasionally peculiar behavior, he quickly won my wife's approval by telling her confidentially over supper at our home that she was one of the most beautiful women he had ever met. She thus had no reservations about my inviting him to read at the university where I taught and stay with us after we moved to Massachusetts.

Aware of the Second Vatican Council's emphasis on lay participation and theologians responsible for its impact on the institutional church, my wife and I were active in the Christian Family Movement. After wrangling an invitation from John Cogley, editor of *Commonweal Magazine*, I attended a major conference sponsored by Robert Hutchins's Center for the Study of Democratic Institutions on the encyclical of John XXIII, "Pacem in Terris." Participants included ambassadors, journalists, scholars, and foreign and domestic dignitaries including Senator William Fulbright, Paul Tillich, Marya Mannes, and Adlai Stevenson. The presentations and discussions at the United Nations and the Hilton Hotel in New York City amounted to a revelation that significantly affected my thinking regarding moral and ethical issues relating to public policy.

Back on campus, a historian arranged a forum focusing on "Pacem in Terris," with faculty members from the history, philosophy, and political science departments responding to my report of the conference. Not surprisingly, after roundly dismissing the conference, they downplayed its significance to the Cold War by relying on arguments consistent with realpolitik and the just war tradition, including increasing US involvement in Vietnam.

In naively taking on the powers and challenging basic assumptions of US policy, I provoked heated responses that left me bloodied but unbowed. If that's the worst that can happen to a person, I thought, with additional homework, I would be ready for the next encounter. In a speech at Indiana State University, David McReynolds of the War Resisters League gave an informed, detailed, and concrete challenge to the war in Southeast Asia. By basing his argument on information available to any thoughtful reader, he dramatized the necessity of reading newspapers and journals other than the popular press. It slowly dawned on me that the old saw about experts in Washington knowing more than ordinary citizens about major issues was simple-minded if not downright dangerous. That realization and additional research led me into a minor career from then on as an antiwar activist.

About the same time, I attended an event sponsored by the American Friends Service Committee, the service wing of the Quakers that opposes war, including the US war in Vietnam. After participating in civil rights demonstrations in the early 1960s, I had seriously considered registering voters in Mississippi but never followed through on the plan.

Teaching literature at Indiana State enabled me to fill in the gaps and, in a sense, to complete an education that I had not received. Living in Terre Haute, the hometown of the great unionist Eugene Debs and frequenting his former residence, I learned much about him and his remarkable life as a labor organizer and influence on American culture. My salary, with extra teaching in the summer, improved our financial status and enabled our family to visit more family in Oklahoma and Minnesota and to travel to New York City to soak up the special ambiance there. Over the next four years, we saw the births of our sons John Keenan and Christopher Page in 1962 and 1964, and I completed the dissertation and oral examination at Duke in the summer before my final year on the Indiana State faculty.

With the hope of moving closer to our families, my wife, Mary Pat, and I began thinking about leaving Terre Haute in favor of greener pastures. Although we had enjoyed life in Terre Haute, since Chicago was within striking distance to the north and the University of Indiana and Brown County to the south, the city itself had a rather frumpy look and disposition with little indication of potential improvement. Also, my teaching assignment as a junior member of a large department was unlikely to include anything beyond introductory courses for many years.

Looking for a full-time teaching position took me to the annual conference of the Modern Language Association in New York, where I signed up for its so-called slave market, as hungry young scholars deemed it. While interviewing with colleges and universities, Mary Pat and I made the most of our time by attending the riotous English review, *Beyond the Fringe,* and, with the idea of writing about Edward Hopper, my favorite American painter, I interviewed with Lloyd Goodrich at the Whitney Museum with its collection of Hopper paintings.

After initially saying I wasn't interested in the job, I went for an interview and received an offer as assistant professor at Assumption College in Worcester, Massachusetts. When the contract arrived, it stipulated I would say nothing contrary to Catholic teaching. Not knowing who would be making the decision about no signature, I returned it unsigned. A month later, I received and signed a contract without the stipulation, a change adopted from then on by the college.

At the end of the school year, Mary Pat, six months' pregnant with twins, and the two older boys went ahead to stay with her family in St. Paul while I packed our belongings, cleared out the Terre Haute house, and looked after Mary Laurel, six, and Christopher, eleven months. After grading seventy-five final exams on our last day in Terre Haute, I loaded our Ford van with suitcases and a baby crib. With Chris in the back and Mary Laurel in the seat beside me, I drove two hundred miles to Galesburg, Illinois, left the car at a friend's house, and boarded the Santa Fe Chief at midnight for Oklahoma City.

Completely exhausted, I fell asleep immediately, but after a few moments of peace, I caught Chris opening a bottle of Bufferin, buffered aspirin he found in my Dopp kit. Watching him every second as I wondered if he'd harmed himself and whether I should pull the chain to stop the train, I got little sleep for the remainder of the trip.

The time with my parents in Oklahoma was a treat, as usual, for us. After a week in Lawton, the three of us boarded the Santa Fe Chief in Oklahoma City for the return to Galesburg, picked up the car, and drove to Minneapolis. Leaving Chris with Mary Pat for their eventual flight to Worcester, Michael, John, Mary Laurel, and I headed east after a few days. En route to Massachusetts, we spent a night with our generous inlaws, the Jolins in Madison, Wisconsin.

Massachusetts, 1965

As if I were sent so that whatever takes place
has meaning because it changes into memory.

—Czeslaw Milosz

Driving across the state line from New York onto the Massachusetts
Turnpike, I expected to find mostly factories and urban sprawl, so the
beautiful stretches of green through the Berkshire Mountains provided a
pleasant surprise. As a Southwesterner who had visited New England only
briefly, Massachusetts struck me initially as somewhat foreign. We spent
the first night in Lee, near Tanglewood, summer home of the Boston
Symphony, and Jacob's Pillow, site of a well-known dance festival. We
continued the following morning on to Worcester, where we felt pleased
by the first sight of our new home in a central location between the college
and downtown.

Living fifteen hundred miles from our families and assimilating a new
culture took some doing, particularly after the twins, Betsy and Anne,
made their entrance at Worcester City Hospital six weeks after we arrived
in the city. Fortunately, Bernard and Mary Farragher had rented a
three-story duplex house for us. Bernie chaired the Assumption
Department of English. Built in 1893, the entire house, which we
occupied, had ten rooms, handsome woodwork, and a basement. Longtime
residents assured us that the city was neither Boston nor New York, which
we soon came to appreciate, despite all it had to offer: ten colleges; rich
literary, industrial, and social history; opportunities to hear poets, public
figures, and good music; and beautiful beaches only an hour or so away.

Within two weeks, I was teaching a graduate course in the poetry of
Milton, sometimes feeling on my way to campus that my years of study had

brought me to a very good place. My fall teaching assignment, two upper division undergraduate courses and a graduate course, constituted an enviable one at a decent salary. And I soon found a small, local community of people involved in the civil rights struggle and a nascent movement against the Vietnam War. After that, stopping the war consumed much of my time and energy outside of teaching and writing as we sponsored events and organized actions throughout New England during the ensuing ten years.

Although a modest college of four hundred male undergraduates, Assumption values teaching. The students wrote competently and appreciated literature and the humanities. Founded in 1905 by the Roman Catholic monastic order, Augustinians of the Assumption, the college had links to the French Canadian community. When I arrived on campus, Assumptionists had embraced the spirit of Vatican II and policies associated with it thus accompanying a fruitful period for Catholic culture, however parochial in some ways. Well-educated clergy knew about European theologians and intellectuals. American writers such as Robert

Michael during his early days at Assumption College, Worcester, Massachusetts

Lowell, Flannery O'Connor, and Mary McCarthy made valuable use of their Catholic experience, even in criticizing it. In a high point of my first year, I joined Robert Fitzgerald, Boylston Professor of Rhetoric at Harvard and O'Connor's friend, on Boston's public television Channel 2, WGBH, to review *Everything that Rises Must Converge,* her collection of short stories. Sally Fitzgerald, Robert's wife and editor of O'Connor's letters, later lectured at Assumption and stayed with us for several days during a winter storm.

Mary Pat and Michael with their family, about 1967, including, from left, front,
Betsy, Anne, Mary, Michael, Chris, and John

While the early years in Worcester proved strenuous for me at Assumption and with various antiwar projects, Mary Pat stayed at home with our six young children. She shepherded them to the grade school just two blocks away. She made lunches and dinners and took the kids grocery shopping, to second-hand stores, and out to lunch at Friendly's or Newport Creamery. I give her a lot of credit in keeping the household together. Mary Pat developed friendships easily, and her friends often came by for visits. Later, she would go to lunch and dinner with her co-workers from the Worcester Public Schools child psychology department and Worcester Children's Friend Society. She has always been a good conversationalist and comes from a long line of Irish-American storytellers.

Mary Pat loves to engage with people, and what begins as "How are you doing?" becomes a longer chat about where someone grew up and how many children they have. Mary Pat has the gift of a casual detective. She is truly interested in other people's lives and their histories. Mary Pat welcomed so many guests, visiting poets, and writers to stay overnight on our third floor.

We were lucky to have a big house which could accommodate friends and family. Bernie Farragher, chair of my department and the best administrator I ever worked for, supported young teachers he hired and introduced policies that benefited the college. Most of the faculty were devoted to teaching, and on Friday afternoons, teachers and administrators gathered in the Salon of la Maison Française for cocktails and conversation. We constituted a small community committed to building a good college with an enlightened, unobtrusive administration and a lively, well-educated young faculty.

The first year nonetheless proved stressful for several reasons. Unfamiliar with New England Catholicism as well as French Canadian culture, I found it surprising that the college required students to attend daily mass and live under restricted dorm rules. My biggest surprise came when I donated Mary McCarthy's novel *The Group* and other contemporary novels to the college library. Deciding that *The Group* wasn't appropriate reading on campus, the head librarian balked at my choice. Fortunately, when Bernie Farragher found out what had happened, he resolved the matter without fanfare.

Other than a priest who occasionally tore down posters advertising speakers against the Vietnam War, the only censor I ran into occurred when I invited Tom and Marjorie Melville in the summer of 1968. Maryknoll missionaries thrown out of Guatemala for working with the poor, the Melvilles had joined the Roman Catholic priests, Daniel Berrigan and Philip Berrigan, and others in burning draft files in the parking lot of the Catonsville, Maryland, draft board two months earlier. Father Louis F. Dion, dean of the college representing the administrative council, wrote to the faculty that the Melvilles would not be offered a forum at Assumption as, he said, it "would be viewed adversely by the chancery." He also referred to "the presence on campus as summer students of a considerable body of sisters (nuns)—some of whom may not be as sophisticated as the Assumption College faculty."

In a letter to the faculty citing American Association of University Professors speakers policy, I questioned the council's barring "certain speakers on campus on the possibility that they might offend" someone. I also questioned its ability to make a judgment about the sophistication of

Daniel Berrigan, left, and Michael

our summer graduate students, including my own." Ironically," I added, "at least twenty percent of the audience at the local YWCA," where the Melvilles subsequently spoke, "was made up of sisters from our summer school." That represented the last time the administrative council prevented a speaker from coming to campus until after my retirement, under a different administration, more than thirty years later.

Meanwhile, I savored other rich and productive aspects of my early years at Assumption. From a distance, in fact, it's difficult to convey the excitement I felt as I drove to the college in the morning. I looked forward to teaching John Milton's "Lycidas," for example, perhaps the greatest lyric in English, or to plunge into *Paradise Lost*, reading passages simply for their sound and majesty. Although Milton and, later, Alexander Pope, Jonathan Swift, and Henry Fielding were not my forte, I leaned on the great editions of and scholarship about their work and, thus, did a credible job of making them available to students. Students participated in lively debates based upon the criticism of T. S. Eliot and William Empson, who often praised the metaphysical poets John Donne and George Herbert at Milton's expense. I wonder if I would have approached Pope's "Pastorals" or "The Rape of the Lock" or John Gay's *The Beggar's Opera* with such enthusiasm—probably so. The students appeared interested, in any event, perhaps sharing a sense of discovery that made whatever poem I discussed my absolute favorite poem at that moment.

Preparing for our final class discussion of *Paradise Lost,* I remember having a sudden sense of the overall architecture and majesty of Milton's epic as well as my awe and gratitude to be engaged in the happy circumstance of reading him with the students. My studies with Samuel Monk at Minnesota had also given me a more subdued but genuine appreciation for the neoclassic period. Reading Pope's "Dunciad" ridiculing the stupidities of eighteenth-century governance seemed absolutely relevant to the behavior of American policy makers as the Vietnam War dragged on. Immersing myself in the period of Enlightenment at that time provided excellent preparation for my later teaching and writing about American literary radicals, particularly Thomas Paine. Meanwhile, I was publishing essays in scholarly publications based on my dissertation after the University of Oklahoma Press turned down my book based on the dissertation.

By the early 1970s, my teaching focused primarily on American literature, especially modern poetry and the 1930s as I arranged for poets and writers, including James T. Farrell and Karl Shapiro, to read on campus, visit classes, and spend the night in our home. Spending time with Farrell and Shapiro, especially, offered an education in itself, since both— generous, unpretentious, and learned—embodied social and literary histories of the period from 1930 to 1970. Although Shapiro received a Pulitzer Prize at a young age while editing the magazines *Poetry* and *Prairie Schooner,* he stayed clear of the eastern literary establishment while teaching at the University of Nebraska and University of California, Davis. Deeply moved by Allen Ginsberg's 1955 *Howl,* Shapiro had written a witty and somewhat subversive commentary on the poem.

In a sense, then, literary history took place before our very eyes, leading to my co-founding the Worcester County Poetry Association, Inc., and *Worcester Review.* I wrote brief surveys focusing on Worcester writers from George Bancroft and Thomas Wentworth Higginson to Stanley Kunitz, Elizabeth Bishop, Charles Olson, and Frank O'Hara. All such undertakings comprised modest initiatives involving local enthusiasts or former undergraduate or graduate students in my classes. Although we had no money to speak of, we had a deep love of poetry and relied on student funding at colleges or from alumni groups for honoraria to visiting writers.

Reading and discussing poems by Robert Frost, Wallace Stevens, Eliot, and William Carlos Williams as well as by Theodore Roethke and Ginsberg, amounted to pleasures that far exceeded my expectations as a teacher. In reading and discussing poems, even those I had known for years, students often revealed aspects I had completely missed. Over the next few years, Robert Bly and John Logan, among others, visited our classes. Denise Levertov read her long poem, "To Stay Alive," once described "not as mere confessional autobiography but as a document of some historical value" that focused on the late 1960s and early 1970s. One year, graduating seniors chose a prose poem by Karl Shapiro for their baccalaureate ceremony. It begins

> Lower the standard: that's my motto.
> Somebody is always putting the food out of reach.
> We're tired of falling off ladders.
> Who says a child can't paint?
> A pro is somebody who does it for money.

the poet Robert Bly with Michael about 1985

My family and I made friends locally and enjoyed New England, particularly tours of the Boston area and brief vacations at the magnificent beach in Ogunquit, Maine. Preparing to teach a course in religion and literature, I enrolled as a post-doctoral student at Harvard Divinity School for courses with Dean Samuel Miller and Harvey Cox, already an international celebrity because of his popular book, *The Secular City*. In the late sixties, the divinity school was a hotbed of scholarly and political activity with visiting theologians of world religions and students and faculty involved in public issues.

In Worcester on Friday nights, The Phoenix, a political forum, sponsored well-known speakers on civil rights and foreign policy and on ecclesiastical and liturgical reforms associated with Vatican II. People gathered at a storefront at 65½ Main Street to hear faculty from nearby colleges and universities, the American Friends Service Committee, and the War Resisters League. Abbie Hoffman, a Worcester native active at The Phoenix, had already established a local reputation for his talent at street theater. Before an audience of right-wing politicos at Worcester Public Library, he had unfurled a wide banner that read, in large letters, "Fuck Communism." After studying at Brandeis University and UC Berkeley and working as a medical supply salesman at the time, he opened a Snick Shop (for SNCC: Student Nonviolent Coordinating Committee) next door to The Phoenix. Snick Shop sold handicrafts from Mississippi to benefit voter registration there. Abbie's local compatriots included Father Bernard Gilgun, a diocesan priest active in the civil rights movement and later chaplain to Worcester's Mustard Seed Catholic Worker. Eventually, in the late sixties, Abbie left for New York and national fame.

As the stupidity and failure of American policy became apparent in Southeast Asia, local citizens began questioning government policy and its consequences, particularly the escalation of troops in Vietnam to half a million. Ken and Stephen Dupuis of Worcester left for Canada to avoid the US draft, and another young man was imprisoned for draft resistance. Philip Goguen from nearby Gardner first read Leo Tolstoy's early twentieth century pamphlet against military conscription when he went AWOL from Fort Dix, New Jersey, to visit his representative in Congress in Washington, DC. Like many others, he sought a discharge from the army on grounds of conscientious objection. The courage of such young men, several of them my students, deepened my opposition to the war.

During Vietnam summer, 1967, Thurston Taylor, director of Worcester Public Library, opened a draft information center at The Phoenix to provide information that, by law, should have been available from the Selective Service System, responsible for administering US conscription into the American military. Soon, local residents and students from Worcester and nearby colleges began picketing buses taking young men to Boston for induction.

Earlier, Barbara Deming of the War Resisters League returned from Vietnam with evidence refuting claims that the US did not use anti-personnel weapons there. Assumption students in the audience stood on their chairs to yell in protest at her information. Within a year, several of them applied for conscientious objection.

Civil disobedience at Arlington Street Church, Boston, by Dr. Benjamin Spock and Reverend William Sloane Coffin Jr., chaplain at Yale, followed by their trials and imprisonment, made a deep impression on me. So did the April 1967 speech of Martin Luther King Jr. at Riverside Church in New York when he reflected his understanding of the origins and history of war and its unpopularity among African Americans.

Boston University's radical historian Howard Zinn, Massachusetts Institute of Technology's radical linguist and historian Noam Chomsky, and members of the Catonsville Nine and Milwaukee Fourteen, prosecuted for burning draft records, all drew large audiences when I invited them to speak locally. Meanwhile, my letters and Op-Ed pieces against the war appeared in the local press. I joined with other concerned citizens who counseled young men trying to make informed decisions about the draft.

Familiar with opposition to World War I by Randolph Bourne, Bertrand Russell, and Eugene Debs, I gradually came to know activists in the same tradition who opposed the Vietnam War, particularly Mulford Sibley, Dorothy Day, and Ammon Hennacy.

A political science professor at the University of Minnesota, Sibley had debated a St. Paul alderman regarding freedom of speech. Sibley maintained that, since the university is a place to debate matters of importance, students have a right to invite anyone they want to speak on campus, including socialists, Communists, or nudists. A lively, thoughtful, though never offensive debater, he attracted large audiences in the Twin Cities and admirers in the wider community. My mother-in-law who lived in St. Paul, for example, regarded him with skepticism until she met him at a family gathering. Having invited him to Indiana when I was there, I arranged for Sibley to speak at Assumption, where he was equally successful. The campus vibrated for several days following his thought-provoking lecture and question and answer period. Historians of nonviolence owe Sibley a debt for his classic 1952 study, *The Quiet Battle,* and an earlier pamphlet, *The Politics of Pacifism.*

I met Dorothy Day in 1964 on my first visit to the Catholic Worker on Christie Street in Manhattan during a "Pacem in Terris" conference at the UN. Within minutes of our introduction, she learned about my interest in Randolph Bourne, whom she had admired during World War I and occasionally quoted in the movement's *Catholic Worker* newspaper. Her subsequent invitation to speak about him at a Friday night clarification of thought at the Worker was my first of many visits there.

When Dorothy spent the night in our daughter's room on the third floor, she asked if she might have a Bufferin and morning cup of coffee. The joke of peace activist and Catholic Worker Ammon Hennacy about Dorothy was that she couldn't start the revolution without coffee and a Bufferin first thing in the morning. Dorothy appreciated whatever we served at mealtime, even if it were only Campbell's beef and barley soup. She demonstrated mindfulness to everything around her, particularly Mary Pat's attentiveness to our six small children. A prayer book discarded from a convent that she gave to Mary Pat carries the inscription, "To pray within distraction. Dorothy Day, April 1971."

Leaving our house to address the New England Catholic Peace Fellowship Conference after asking if she looked presentable enough to appear in public and lightly brushing the front of her blouse, Dorothy had some difficulty in her eighth decade climbing into the passenger seat of our Ford van. Although she spoke of nervousness before speaking at the college, the audience was, as always, fully attentive once she began speaking. Afterward, she sat in our living room among listeners including Assumption student Fran Anthes and a journalist from Worcester's *Catholic Free Press* newspaper.

Dorothy also graciously accepted invitations to go out for coffee when I visited her in New York. On a fellowship at Columbia in 1976, I welcomed an opportunity to celebrate the November 8 birthday we shared, her seventy-ninth and my forty-third, at Mary House in Lower Manhattan.

After we first met, Dorothy gave Ammon our Worcester address and phone number, so he phoned me before he and his wife, Joan Thomas, dropped by our house. My first sight of Joan came when she stuck her head through the front doorway to ask me if we had a hundred-watt light bulb, which she needed to read music at the piano. Since we indeed had a piano, our one valuable piece of furniture, she proceeded to murder Chopin for the next three days. One is grateful to her, nonetheless, for taking good care of Ammon in his later years and faithfully distributing his privately-printed books which, as Dorothy Day said, include one of the most moving accounts of prison life ever published.

In his early seventies when we first met, Ammon left me completely exhausted after his visits to our home, having filled every moment with lectures at The Phoenix and area colleges, demonstrations in support of the Catonsville Nine, appearances on Joe Hyder's radio show, and visits with Catholic Worker friends in the area. My favorite time, however, happened when he reminisced about his incredibly eventful life as a Christian anarchist and war resister, including his imprisonment during World War I in Atlanta federal prison with Alexander Berkman, Emma Goldman's lover and compatriot.

Dorothy Day, top, in 1971 with students in the Trues' living room and, bottom, with Roland Werme of Douglas, Massachusetts.

During the 1960s, he maintained a Joe Hill house of hospitality in Salt Lake City, when the folk singer Utah Phillips, a homeless veteran of the Korean conflict, lived there. Daily, Ammon made the rounds of supermarkets begging food. He protested against capital punishment at the state capital. A gold mine of information about American history, Ammon associated with the Catholic Worker after he met Dorothy, when she spoke in Milwaukee in the 1930s. Ammon admired her inordinately as a genuine radical and wrote about her in both his *The Book of Ammon*, 1955, and *The One Man Revolution in America*, 1970.

Ammon and Dorothy loved telling stories on one another. He told me that, once as they walked through the Bowery, Dorothy showed him where she had slept with Mike Gold, a popular Communist journalist. Dorothy admired Ammon's courage but thought him unnecessarily contentious when he criticized the clergy, including Cardinal Francis Spellman of New York, whom he referred to as "fat-assed Spellman." Ammon picketed the cardinal on his return to LaGuardia after the cardinal blessed cannons in Korea. But Dorothy also quickly pointed out that Ammon was the first person to give up his bed when someone arrived late at night at the Worker. A remembrance of him shortly after his death, my first article for *Commonweal*, the Catholic magazine, acknowledged my love for him. Half a century later, I feel the same way because of his genuine goodness, wit, intelligence, and courage, and because he taught me most of what I know about American radical history and nonviolence.

On a trip to New York in the mid 1960s, I visited the offices of the Catholic Peace Fellowship near Wall Street soon after Jim Forest and Tom Cornell co-founded it. Cornell, Forest, and David McReynolds, with A. J. Muste and Dorothy Day standing by, burned their draft cards at Union Square in November 1965 in what the sociologist Gordon Zahn called "the great Catholic conspiracy against the war." Clergy and laity, including Daniel Berrigan, Philip Berrigan, Tom Lewis, and six other men and women later burned draft files in Catonsville, Maryland, on May 17, 1968. After invading a draft board housed in a Knights of Columbus hall, they torched the files in the parking lot, using homemade napalm. They said prayers and sang hymns while they waited for arrest. Trials and imprisonment awaited many resisters who committed civil disobedience throughout the country. Daniel Berrigan's prize-winning play, *The Trial of the Catonsville Nine,* translated into many languages, drew more people into the movement, particularly Catholics who had initially supported the war.

In the summer of 1968, as we drove through Chicago on our way home from Minnesota, my family and I heard reports of demonstrations, riots, and police repression at the Democratic National Convention. Several years later, I visited the courtroom during the Chicago Eight trials involving Abbie Hoffman and David Dellinger. In Worcester, the librarian Dan Dick and I initiated a chapter of Clergy and Laity against the War in Vietnam, while Reverend Paul Henniges, a Unitarian minister, and Annabel Wolfson, a former nurse with a Mennonite background, initiated the Interfaith Center for Draft Information, co-sponsored by the Catholic Diocese of Worcester, the Jewish Federation, and the Worcester County Ecumenical Council.

Visiting schools and churches to speak with guidance counselors and students, I served as Annabel's front man by introducing the topic before she answered their detailed questions about draft laws and regulations. Apparently knowing more than most people in Washington, she regularly challenged contradictory rulings by local and state offices of the Selective Service System. Catholics, for example, often were denied conscientious objector classification when draft board members mistakenly told them that their religion did not support their claim. Fortunately, Worcester's Bishop Bernard J. Flanagan testified before a Congressional hearing that, were he a young man, he would apply for conscientious objector status. Since the draft law enabled the president to call up hundreds of thousands of recruits without permission of Congress, I continued to oppose the draft, later initiating the Massachusetts Council to Repeal the Draft.

In spite of the public's increased opposition to the Vietnam War, editorials and cartoons supported the war in the local newspaper owned by the proprietor of local arms-component manufacturer Wyman-Gordon and charter member of the John Birch Society. Although young reporters covering demonstrations gradually became knowledgeable about its history, editors at the *Telegram and Gazette* seemed to go out of their way to ridicule antiwar activists. The newspaper arrogantly and ignorantly lampooned the activists while evidently dismissing hard evidence against America's involvement.

On one occasion, when I wrote a letter to the owner, Robert Stoddard, arguing that management had failed to provide local citizens with a newspaper they deserved, the owner, to the surprise of many, responded. In my second letter, when I mentioned editors' refusal to provide draft information, he wrote back that he was not interested in carrying on a correspondence with me. Meanwhile, my articles and reviews appeared in underground newspapers and other publications, some of them gathered in my 1971 book, *Should the Catholic College Survive?* and other impertinent questions. I stole most of the good ideas in the polemical essays from Paul Goodman's popular book, *Compulsory Mis-education and the Community of Scholars*.

In 1968, my family and some friends, mainly from Catholic backgrounds, initiated the Floating Parish of Worcester, a liturgical

the 1970s Floating Parish of Worcester

introduction to the brochure of the Floating Parish of Worcester
" . . . to provide, for people who hold certain values sacred, an opportunity for
common worship . . .
. . . to educate themselves and their children in the best way they can concerning
Judaeo-Christian belief and practice . . .
. . . to build a community that gives form to its spiritual values . . . "

GENERAL PROCEDURES

THE FLOATING PARISH is a voluntary association, and as such depends upon its participants to offer what they can of themselves and their goods for the commonweal. There is no "membership," and a participant is anyone who feels that the parish can respond to his need and that he can share in its concerns. We hope that the many and varied talents which the participants possess will be offered to all; for we have discovered that the Floating Parish thrives only so long as the outpouring of talent and involvement continues to be expressed.

I. Scheduling

A schedule is customarily set up for two-or-three month periods, indicating the place and hour of meeting and those in charge of the children.

II. Organization Meetings

These policy and planning meetings are held about every 3 months in order to discuss our past experiences and to set out future directions. There are no officers or official leaders and everyone is welcome.

III. Specific Responsibilities

A. The host family opens their home for worship. They arrange for the celebrant and select the music with assistance from any other people in the parish, as needed. The hosts provide the bread and wine, the related vessels and effects for the communion service. They serve the coffee, children's beverage, and pastry for the social hour after the service.

B. The form and content of worship is determined by the nature of the participants, the prior preparation of the celebrant with the host family, and the actual experience of the service itself.

We have found it advisable for the host family to discuss the anticipated service with the invited celebrant in advance, to allow adequate time for reflection and preparation.

We seek to call out the best in all of us and expect that such results will come from worship that is imaginatively conceived and carried out by all involved. We do not seek to impose any rigid forms or customs, nor do we intend that the integrity of the celebrant or congregation be violated or impinged upon; we hope that he or she can relate to us and we to him sincerely and meaningfully.

general procedures of the Floating Parish of Worcester

experiment of people who gathered on Sundays in homes and public parks. Initially, Catholic priests, including Father Daniel Berrigan, acted as celebrants, with Protestant and Jewish clergy fulfilling the role later on. Although the local bishop bragged outside the diocese about the lay initiative, the diocesan chancery sent spies to report on the goings on, which they referred to as "the underground church." The media took particular interest in the Floating Parish, never shy about its public witness, which resembled the Community of the Living Spirit in Wisconsin and the Slant Movement initiated in England by the British scholars Terry Eagleton and Brian Wicker. In addition to traveling around Central Massachusetts, the Floating Parish celebrated Sunday liturgy just outside the gate of Federal Correctional Institution in Danbury, Connecticut, where Daniel Berrigan and Philip Berrigan were incarcerated after the Catonsville action.

As the antiwar movement gathered strength, Worcester became something of a center for protest and resistance. Students at Clark University, where I taught as a visiting professor in various departments, organized buses to Washington for demonstrations and canvassed Worcester voters door-to-door to ask their opinions about the war. Victor Reinstein, a Clark sophomore, organized an effective sit-in in April 1970 "according to strict Gandhian principles," as he said, that involved eight undergraduates, a Clark sociology professor, and me.

We gathered at 5:30 AM on April 4, 1970, a block from the draft board in downtown Worcester and walked nervously to the office on the sixth floor where we sat down and waited for federal employees to arrive for work. On the street below, with observers from the American Civil Liberties Union, friends passed out leaflets explaining what we did and why. Police arrived, first of all to warn and then to arrest us. My doggerel verse at the time described what happened next:

> Tiered people watched, as the kind police
> Apologized their way to jail
> And carried twelve bodies seven flights down,
> Some male and some female.

After that, a paddy wagon took us to the Worcester County Jail and House of Correction in West Boylston a few blocks from the arrest.

"Imprisonment is," I wrote to my students,
a pretty fast education for a petty bourgeois, the food greasy and the
routine deadening, the place filled with young people who are, like
their counterparts on the outside, fun to talk to.

Going to Sunday mass at the jail was something of a revelation as well.
The priest, regarded by inmates as a "religious screw," gave sermons on
obeying the law. "People on the outside have done far worse than you," he
said, "but the one difference between them and you is that they're
smarter—they didn't get caught."

As Dostoevsky once observed, "the degree of civilization in a society
can be judged by entering its prisons."

Our jailing provoked sympathetic protests, especially after the US
invaded Cambodia, with an outburst of activity throughout the city as two
hundred people, including faculty from area colleges, were arrested during
demonstrations. Father Joe LeBrand, the Holy Cross chaplain, hurriedly
left a faculty meeting in order to join other protesters eventually arrested
en masse. Such occurrences, including an attack on the Reserve Officers
Training Corps building by the Revolutionary Student Union at Holy
Cross, seem almost unbelievable fifty years later. So does my memory of a
student then, who later campaigned for a reactionary Republican governor,
walking down Main Street just ahead of me chanting, "One, two, three,
four; we don't want your fuckin' war."

At our trial, in his unsuccessful defense, Attorney Burton Chandler
praised our decision to accept a jail sentence rather than pay a fine. It "was
in the highest form of American tradition—civil disobedience," he said,
and "stood in the eyes of the system higher than the courts of law (the
defendants) appeared before. I am quite proud to represent these people."

Supportive colleagues at Assumption covered my classes while I was in
jail, and our elderly landlady, Agnes Reidy, quietly called Mary Pat over to
her back porch one morning to give her a pint of cream and twenty dollars.
While I was incarcerated, Mary Pat and the children came by and waved to
me from the courtyard below, and a number of clergy visited us, indicating
their support. When Reverend Gordon Torgersen, minister of the First

at the US Capitol, Michael and Jim Noonan mount a protest of the Vietnam War

Baptist Church, came by to see me, the sheriff questioned him at length before allowing him to visit my cell. Since Gordon visited ordinary criminals without such harassment, he was rather shocked by the sheriff's questioning his visiting someone committed to peace. During our conversation in my cell, Gordon invited me to join him in a dialogue sermon on nonviolent civil disobedience the following Sunday after my release. I did so even after a prominent benefactor of his church urged Gordon to cancel the event.

Meanwhile, students from Worcester Polytechnic Institute, Assumption, Holy Cross, Worcester State, and Clark marched from their campuses to city hall for large, round-the-clock demonstrations. Colleges canceled final examinations, and local officials, unlike those at Kent State, responded reasonably to protests as the war continued and casualties increased. Soon after the draft board sit-in, I traveled to Pendle Hill, the Quaker retreat center in Philadelphia, for more detailed and disciplined training in nonviolence in sessions led by Bayard Rustin and Glenn Smiley, who had counseled Martin Luther King Jr. during the 1955 Montgomery campaign.

Several well-known poets who publicly opposed the war supported those of us involved in the local movement. They included Robert Bly, who co-founded Poets Against the War in Vietnam, with David Ray, and committed civil disobedience before then Vice-President Hubert Humphrey at a ceremony in Manhattan. Accepting the National Book Award for his collection, *Light Around the Body*, Bly gave the check accompanying it to a young man, Michael Kempton, and encouraged him to resist the draft. Denise Levertov read in Worcester again about the time that her husband, the novelist Mitchell Goodman, was arrested for supporting young resisters who burned their draft cards on the Boston Common. Stanley Kunitz, who returned frequently to Worcester, his native city, joined Robert Lowell and other poets to boycott an event at the White House, in protest against President Johnson's ongoing war.

In spring 1971, Bly, Levertov, and Kunitz launched the Worcester Poetry Festival at the Worcester Public Library. The impetus for the series

Robert Bly, left, co-founder of Poets Against the War in Vietnam, and Michael

invitation to 1974 public appearance of the poet Denise Levertov

was a meeting with Dr. Sam Bachrach, a local internist, whom Gordon
Kierney, owner of the famous Grolier Bookshop at Harvard Square, had
told me about. Sam and his wife, Lillian, contributed the $450 that
enabled us to invite Bly, Levertov, and Kunitz to open the series. Fran
Quinn initiated "The Worcester Poetry Festival of the Air," on WICN
and *Worcester Review* began publishing a year later. Aware of my
limitations as an editor, I "retired" after the first issue, which may explain
why it's still going strong forty years later. Subsequent issues, edited by
Rodger Martin, have focused on writers either native to or long resident in
the region–Charles Olson, Elizabeth Bishop, Frank O'Hara, Robert
Cormier, and Etheridge Knight, who later initiated the Free People's
Poetry Workshop.

At that time, poetry readings were less common than they became later,
and few writers except Allen Ginsberg expected to sell more than two
thousand copies of a book. Gradually, WCPA and its audience built a
good reputation among poets, since we distributed hundreds of handsome
poetry broadsides prior to a reading and made books available for sale and
autographing afterward. X. J. Kennedy told audiences that next to San
Francisco and New York, Worcester had the best poetry series in the US,

WORCESTER POETRY FESTIVAL

1973 - 1974 Series

Presented by the Worcester County Poetry Association and sponsored by the Worcester Public Library, Friends of the Worcester Public Library, the Massachusetts Council on the Arts and Humanities, and individual contributions.

THE WORCESTER COUNTY POETRY ASSOCIATION— A CREATIVE AWAKENING

Founded in 1971, and incorporated in 1972 as a nonprofit organization, the Worcester County Poetry Association is governed by a board of members who contribute their time to plan a series of readings, correspond with interested writers, and handle all publicity and arrangements to bring live poetry to the Worcester community.

The maintenance and expansion of the activities of the Worcester County Poetry Association depends on the assistance, creative and financial, of individuals interested not only in the art of poetry, but also in the cultural development of Worcester County. In this effort, the Association welcomes the contribution of ideas, planning help, and financial assistance. All donations to the Association, as a nonprofit organization, are tax deductible.

All inquiries should be addressed to:

The Worcester County Poetry Association, Inc.
P.O. Box 16
Worcester, MA   01613

brochure of the 1973-1974 series of the
Worcester Poetry Festival

while Galway Kinnell, originally from Providence, wrote that "Worcester did feel to me, when I was there, like a kind of Athens, . . . because poetry seemed to be part of the normal life of the city."

Robert Bly, especially popular with local audiences, read in the city once a year, supported the Association and generously read for my classes at Assumption and when I taught seven summers at the Upper Midwest Writers Conference, near his cabin in Northern Minnesota. Denise Levertov invited us to her home in East Boston, befriended Mary Pat and on one visit delighted our children by pirouetting on the back of our living room sofa. In 1975, she taught a writing workshop at Assumption, which included young poets later awarded national prizes for their work, including Chris Gilbert, John Hodgen, and Mary Fell. The previous two years, through a National Endowment of the Arts program administered by the Association, young writers had taught poetry workshops in area high schools, with Galway Kinnell, Michael Harper, and David Ignatow as mentors at that time.

WCPA helped to reconcile Stanley Kunitz and his hometown of Worcester, which he formerly drove out of his way to avoid. On his eightieth birthday, the association's president, Carle Johnson, organized a week-long celebration involving David Ignatow and Richard Wilbur, as well as Gregory Orr and Louise Gluck, his former students, who read at various locations around the city. David McKay, a WPI faculty member, set several Kunitz poems to music for a performance at the Worcester Art Museum Renaissance Court, after I nervously read the poems to a large audience, including the author. Kunitz also befriended the Stockmals, who lived in his childhood home, the scene of his poem, "The Pear Tree," published in the *New Yorker*. His essay about growing up in Worcester served as the introduction to my *Worcester Poets, with notes toward a literary history,* 1972, and is reprinted in his collected essays.

Arranging readings and providing hospitality for poets and writers over the years inevitably influenced my teaching, writing, and my public and private life. Certain encounters remain vivid in memory: Joseph Brodsky reading poems in Russian, then giving my colleague, Tom

Puchalsky, a balalaika made by students from his native country; Adrienne Rich, at our dining room table, signing an early collection shortly before receiving the Pulitzer Prize for *Diving into the Wreck;* William Stafford, wearing my son's cowboy boots, too large for him, and traipsing through two feet of snow to a coffee shop near our house; Robert Bly, in our entryway, surrounded by groupies, spinning around to show his Mexican serape; Denise Levertov raising her fist acknowledging the cheers at a huge Clark University auditorium at the time of Kent State and riding a small scooter across campus: she lent the scooter to our son, Christopher; Michael Dennis Brown's sadness on coming down to breakfast, after we learned about the death of James Wright; Seamus Heaney, and other Irish poets dining at Mike and Julie O'Shea's table before reading at Assumption; Muriel Rukeyser's wide-eyed expression as she left the bus from New York as she retold about the Molly Bloom sequence she had seen the night before, saying "Molly is all of us." Shortly afterward, she gave a stunning reading before a large audience at the Worcester Public Library, and, later, at a conference of the New England College English Association at Assumption.

Similar flashbacks from that period, resembling film moving fast forward, include Daniel Berrigan arriving at Holy Cross and pointing to a row of vacant chairs, "I see a number of Jesuit brothers are here." Kenneth Koch being cheered by a raucous, wine-drenched crowd, after arriving late for a reading on campus; a reactionary teacher arguing that Father Berrigan, recently out of jail, shouldn't be allowed to speak on campus; my thinking, as Czeslaw Milosz read at Worcester State, that perhaps I agreed with Levertov "that he was the greatest poet of our time"; the look of amazement on my students' faces in the contemporary poetry course, as Robert Kelly, at the front of the classroom, planted a passionate kiss on his gorgeous partner, before giving a brilliant lecture on Ezra Pound; David Ignatow saying on a ride from Quabbin Regional High School, Barre, to Worcester, about how "wild" the woody scene looked to a New Yorker; Louise Clifton, sitting in the living room telling stories about her early childhood; Donald Hall regaling dinner guests at the Castle Restaurant before his reading at the Barre Public Library; my son Michael, eight years old, in a crowded living room, asking Stanley Kunitz the question on everyone's mind, "Why did you become a poet?"; John Logan reading "Picnic," later chosen by Joan and Frank Cassidy for their anniversary celebration and Chris and Angie for their wedding ceremony beside a lake in Minnesota.

Leaning on the American Friends Service Committee staff in Cambridge, Sister Elizabeth Hillman, RC; Kathy Knight, Jim Noonan, and I initiated the New England Catholic Peace Fellowship (NECPF), which attracted four hundred people at the first conference at Holy Cross and Assumption colleges. In addition to Dorothy Day as the principal speaker, members of the Milwaukee Fourteen offered workshops in nonviolence training. As Catholics on the AFSC Committee, Kathy, Jim, and I realized that we needed to work among our own religious community, since the Quakers could take care of themselves, so over the next twenty-five years, we gathered on campuses and at organizations throughout the region, with presentations by then Father James Carroll, chaplain, Boston University, and Dolores Huerta, United Farm Workers, until the organization folded into Massachusetts Pax Christi chaired by Jane Morrissey, SSJ. Several local activists later joined the Plowshares, Jonah House, and Catholic Workers communities after being jailed for civil disobedience at weapons manufacturers.

Living more than a thousand miles from our families, my wife, Mary Pat, our six children, and I depended upon and received help from Worcester friends (it takes a village). Few people had the courage to invite the eight of us or our friends, Marjory and Dan Dick and their nine children, to dinner, so we invited one another, all nineteen of us gathered at their home for Thanksgiving and ours for Easter.

On occasional weekends, Julie and Mike O'Shea invited several colleagues and wives to their home for gourmet meals, with Manhattans before and appropriate wines accompanying the meals. David Christianson, a born mimic and brilliant linguist, provided the entertainment by "doing the faculty senate in many voices" as recordings of "A Night at the Proms" and "Rule Britannica" boomed from the next room. David Christiansen had a wealth of material to draw from, accurately conveying the sense and nonsense of faculty meetings and the academy as his audience around the dinner table cried with laughter. Tom Puchalsky railed at the rest of us for not reading Russian, Polish, and Central European writers, such as Marina Tsvetaveva and Zbigniew Herbert who were obviously superior to the English, American, French, and Spanish poets we were reading. When the group gathered around the piano after dinner at our home, the children eventually called from upstairs that our singing kept them awake. One night at Puchalsky's, the police arrived after neighbors complained about the rowdy bunch next door.

In summer, our family spent a week in Ogunquit, Maine, only a two hour ride from Worcester, renting a cabin that we could afford from the Weares, longtime residents. A short walk from Perkins Cove, their house had room for all eight of us and occasional visitors, including my parents. The children played for hours in the small pools on the beach, when the tide was out. Ogunquit's relative quiet and magnificent scenery, with leisurely walks along the magnificent white-sandy beach, seemed a long way from our work-a-day lives at home. At that time, before interstate highways made it easily accessible to tourists from beyond New England, the beach and the town were relatively uncrowded.

In 1972, George and Louise Garrelts moved to the city after their marriage. That summer, Mary Pat suffered a heart attack and received the last sacraments from our friend, Father Frank Scollen. Telling the older children, particularly Mary Laurel, about their mother being in Worcester City Hospital, after our spending a summer afternoon at the lake is a painful memory still. Fortunately, Mary Pat recovered, after a stay at Peter Bent Brigham Hospital, Boston, and a respite of several weeks. Denise Levertov visited her once she returned home, calling softly, as she descended the stairs, "Mary Pat, I love you." While our children were growing up, I spent many hours in hospital waiting rooms with bleeding or feverish children and at the office of the superintendent of schools explaining why one of them refused to attend a particular school.

In addition to teaching classes, working as a school psychologist, caring for our family, and participating in the peace movement, my wife opened our home with me to friends, poets, activists, hippies, and students with pony tails and variously attired. On several occasions, an older woman next door, with a questionable reputation and Vatican connections, accused us of making a ghetto out of the neighborhood. One evening, as my son John and I sat on the bottom stair leading to the second floor, fifty or more revelers from *AVATAR*, a Boston psychedelic magazine facing obscenity charges, filled our dining room with musicians on top of the dining room table and the air pungent with marijuana or whatever other current substance. When John was about eight, he confronted Father Berrigan as he sat at our breakfast table with the question: "Well, what kind of trouble are you up to now?" However that mélange of visitors struck our children, they seemed to carry on as if it were normal. Meanwhile, they passed the neighborhood paper route from the older to a younger member of the family, and our dog, Rocky, became more familiar than any of them regarding where to deliver the newspaper.

Efforts to end the war in Vietnam absorbed much of my time during the late 1960s and early 1970s. Russell Johnson, former director of American Friends' Service Committee conference and seminar in Southeast Asia, built the peace movement in New England. One of the best speakers I have ever heard, Russell traveled widely, with a selection of books on peacemaking and social justice, meeting students and church groups and speaking to Rotary and Kiwanis clubs. In addressing controversial issues, he held an audience, however unsympathetic it might be to that point of view. During the discussion period, he answered relevant or hostile questions. No one ever asked Russell a "dumb" question. As a consequence of his extraordinary leadership, several remarkable activists, including Frances Crowe of Northampton, eventually initiated American Friends Service Committee regional offices on their own.

Public reaction to my involvement with National Council to Repeal the Draft sometimes provoked fierce reactions, leading to my receiving postcards telling me to go back to the Soviet Union. One reader, for example, copied my letter to the editor about the draft information service to the local newspapers, scrawled TREASON across it, FIGHT COMMUNISM EVERYWHERE at the bottom, and the word QUISLING over my name. Speaking in American Legion halls and elsewhere, I was sometimes the only person in the room calling for the end of the draft. I testified before the senate armed services committee, co-chaired by Senator Barry Goldwater. One of the surprises of my life was picking up the morning newspaper in 1973 with a headline saying that the draft had been put on standby.

Sometimes, our improvisational actions against the war had limited impact. As inexperienced and sometimes naïve resisters, we underestimated powerful forces in the Pentagon, Congress, and arms industry responsible for US foreign policy. The persistence of the movement and courage of draft and war resisters, including men in the service, resulted in two important changes in policy. Although prepared to do so, Nixon did not use nuclear weapons in Vietnam and deactivated the draft. Four decades later, however, in her 1966 poem "Life at War," as Levertov wrote, "the same war continues." Only gradually did I realize the war's negative effect on young people, even those not directly involved in it. Contrary to "spitting image" accusations influenced by scenes in a film released ten years later and to what some people claimed, members of the antiwar movement treated returning veterans with care. When I later joined former veterans in speaking about the war years later, we had much in common, in spite of our differences in experience.

a protest cartoon from Michael's collection

Looking back on my antiwar efforts with some satisfaction, I regret not explaining to my children my reasons, as well as underlying values, for my behavior. Mary Pat ended up handling more than her share of child-rearing, and she, rather than I, should have written about our trying to teach peacemaking in the family and to explain, as one of my friends said, "what we were trying to do and how it went wrong." Mary Pat also suffered the consequences of my antiwar activity when the superintendent of schools refused to hire her as a school psychologist, after she was recommended five times for the position. He apparently never forgave my accepting an invitation to speak against the war on behalf of the senior class at Doherty High School, as he stood on the stage beside me.

In the mid-seventies, George Garrelts, David O'Brien, and I agreed to teach an upper class course in religion at Mt. St. Charles Academy, Woonsocket, Rhode Island, soon learning why everyone else had failed at it. As in many Catholic schools, religion courses were not a high priority, and about the time we got the students interested in our approach, the administration excused hockey players from exams. At the end of the year, the three of us agreed that our year's effort achieved no redeeming social or educational value whatsoever.

Teaching literature at Assumption and colleges nearby, meanwhile, led to my learning what had escaped me during my less than stunning performance as a student. Almost without realizing it, writing became important to me, initially in letters to the editor and book reviews and eventually in magazines and scholarly journals. In 1972, Margaret Thorbeck, Upper Midwest Writers Conference, invited me to teach at a summer writers conference among established poets, novelists, and children's writers in Bemidji, Minnesota. Although I had published only reviews and essays, teaching a graduate Workshop on the Teaching of English at Assumption provided background and experience that was useful in courses for writers and experienced teachers. The stipend for summer teaching enabled us to afford a family vacation, with all eight of us driving thirteen hundred miles to Minnesota and visiting relatives and friends along the way. Giving the children allowances to spend as they wished helped to make it a pleasant trip and infinitely preferable to complaints about their having nothing to do at

Bemidji State
University

10th
Upper Midwest
Writers' Conference

July 17-28, 1978

*1978 brochure of the
Upper Midwest Writers Conference*

home. One dark night when our car broke down near Duluth, two young men drove the eight of us the remaining two hundred miles in their van, carpeted wall to wall, with rock music blaring. The children were delighted.

At our cabin on Lake Bemidji, near the source of the Mississippi River, farmers on vacation from Midwestern states taught my sons how to fish. Robert Bly, who spent summers with his wife, Carol, and their four children at nearby Lake Kabekona visited us and my writing classes. Over the next seven summers, Carol and I became friends, teaching together, corresponding, and visiting one another. By the time of her death in 2005, her work had attracted a wide audience, particularly her first book, *Letters from the Country,* a kind of twentieth-century Walden, and a film, *Rachel River,* based upon her remarkable short stories in *Backbone.*

One of the most vital, talented people I have known, Carol enlivened any conversation or gathering with her original stories, flights of imagination, wit, and wide learning. In a representative aside, she might launch into an extended description, for example, of how the brain works, and the second movement of a Beethoven sonata. At her home on Sturgeon Lake, near Duluth, she planted long rows of strawberry plants, and prepared generous meals for visitors. Although she valued her education at Phillips Andover Academy and Wellesley College, she excoriated some of her classmates from "empire schools" who went on to work for the CIA or arms manufacturers. She couldn't believe that anyone with an education resembling her own could, in conscience, fall so low. Characters in her stories often suffer similar moral lapses in their public lives, and her anthology, *Changing the Bully Who Rules the World,* and rabble-rousing pamphlets exhort her fellow alumni and alumnae to encourage nurturing ethical behavior.

Time with Carol was never dull, as anyone knows who has read her marvelous novel, *Shelter Half,* 2005, published posthumously. A powerful moral tale set in rural Minnesota, it dramatizes the effects of the military-industrial complex on the moral lives of residents, in a manner that is both humorous and deeply serious.

After two weeks at the Upper Midwest Writers Conference, our family spent time with Mary Pat's relatives in the Twin Cities, but also with longtime friends and writers, including J. F. Powers, Regents Professor at St. John's University, Collegeville, Minnesota. As a graduate student at Minnesota, I had met Jim when I drove Anne Fremantle, a well-known Catholic writer, to Collegeville for a talk in the mid fifties. At that time, he relegated "the driver" (me) to the entryway while he and Fremantle engaged in a "serious" discussion. Later when we became friends, I enjoyed reminding him of his earlier condescension toward a struggling graduate student. After a particularly memorable presentation at the writers conference, he and his wife, Betty Wahl, invited us to visit them on our way from Bemidji to Minneapolis. Another time, thirteen of us, eight in our family and five in my sister-in-law's family, the Lanphers, piled into Jim and Betty's home after a fierce thunderstorm. We were treated to a splendid home-cooked meal, including raspberry pie from berries in their garden, which was almost as memorable as the scotch and conversation. Another time I dropped by, Jim's old friend, Gordon Zahn, author of *Solitary Witness: The Life and Death of Franz Jaggerstatter* and *German Catholics and Hitler's War,* had just arrived from Massachusetts. The conversation between them that evening gave one a sense of what it must have been like to join Samuel Johnson and James Boswell at a London tavern in the eighteenth century.

Many details about family life during those years escape me, although vivid scenes emerge occasionally, in a kaleidoscope of images: my sitting on the basement floor stuffing one, two, three dead kittens in a plastic bag to prevent the kids from discovering them; cautioning the children against telling neighbors or schoolmates about the AWOL soldier, whom we were trying to get to Canada on the QT; a thoughtful neighbor arriving at our front door with one of the children woozy and wobbly from a football game or the police standing at the front door with another child on the lam from the nearby skid yard; receiving the news at a writers conference, just before my scheduled talk, that our relatively-new used car had been totaled, although no one was hurt; and discovering the morning after his arrival that Michael and a friend had ridden a motorcycle eighteen hundred miles from Oklahoma University to Worcester.

When the war finally ended in 1975, my professional life became even more rewarding. By that time, teaching a popular course on the 1930s-Hemingway, Steinbeck, and Orwell as well as the poems of Dylan Thomas, Karl Shapiro, and Theodore Roethke, I met Utah Phillips, who visited the class and taught more history in an hour than most academics could convey in a full semester. Perhaps I romanticize that time (What would my former students say about it?), but I must mention the pleasures of my early years at Assumption.

Slowly gaining confidence as a teacher, I came to realize that if I loved my students and my subject, other things would take care of themselves. And how could one not love them, because of their beauty and resourcefulness. An entry in my journal about that time, though it says nothing about the context, may have been prompted by my response to a favorite student: "It's such a pleasure to think for a while about someone I love, feeling the soul go out of itself in true disinterestedness to want to appreciate, to do something for, to bless, to encourage; to harbor in one's heart as a treasure; to wonder about and to hope for, yet to hold back so as not to overwhelm, to remain vulnerable, even put oneself at risk, while allowing the other person freedom to choose or to turn away, though hoping for a gesture, a nod, an affirmation."

A special boon for my class in American writing of the 1930s was the opportunity to arrange an exhibit of paintings and photographs at the Worcester Art Museum, as I had done previously with the *Dial* Collection, on the fiftieth anniversary of the Catholic Worker. Rita Corbin, longtime artist for the Catholic Worker, and Tamar Hennessey, Dorothy Day's daughter, attended the opening of Catholic Worker exhibition. Fritz Eichenberg, who donated work to the Catholic Worker newspaper after Dorothy Day invited him to do so, conducted a memorable workshop in printmaking and drawing. The program, directed by Virginia Raguin, Holy Cross art historian and funded by the National Endowment for the Arts, enabled teachers from area colleges to plan exhibits related to their classes. It involved selecting works from the museum's rich collection of prints, paintings, sculpture, and photographs, writing labels for them, and arranging appropriate poetry readings, lectures, and receptions.

Scofield Taylor of Worcester published *Dial* magazine, but at his death, his collection of contemporary art and manuscripts went, unfortunately, to the Metropolitan Museum in New York. Members of the Worcester County Poetry Association read poems by Yeats, Eliot, Williams, Pound, and e. e. cummings, first published in *Dial*, at the Metropolitan's exhibition of work from the *Dial* collection. Those exhibits, in elegant surroundings, brought both the art and poetry to life in a special way, to the benefit of the teacher most of all. Eventually, I enrolled in and delighted in studio courses at the museum, where we amateurs were encouraged to copy works by Rembrandt and Robert Rauschenberg.

By 1976, after chairing the English department for two years, during which time my teaching deteriorated, a National Endowment for the Humanities Fellowship at Columbia University offered a welcome respite and an opportunity to regain my enthusiasm for American literature. The seminar, Revolution and American literature with the distinguished scholar of American studies Sacvan Bercovitch, deepened my knowledge of American literary and social history, particularly through his amazing lectures on the Puritans, the work of Hawthorne and Melville, and insights drawn from the anthropologist Victor Turner. Without realizing it at the time, the seminar would be a phenomenal contribution to my later helping to initiate an American literature program at Nanjing University in China and, after that, to write about the history of nonviolence in the US from the seventeenth century to the present.

Professor Bercovitch also arranged a stunning array of events, beginning with members of the seminar visiting the Statue of Liberty on July 4, guest lectures by major scholars and critics from this country and abroad throughout the year and an afternoon with the Carnegie Hall dance group loyal to the memory of Isadora Duncan. Through the generosity of a friend, I had a free apartment near Columbia for the academic year, or at least for midweek during that year, since I traveled back and forth to Worcester on the weekend.

Although my primary interests were aesthetic, because of my indebtedness to the New Criticism, my work with American studies scholars such as Charles Fenton and later Sacvan Bercovitch gave me more familiarity with the social and historical roots of literature and political movements. That proved particularly helpful after 1980 when it became necessary to reinvent myself as a quasi-social scientist teaching peace, conflict, and nonviolence studies. My brother Herb often lectured as a motivational speaker combining psychology, humor, and graphics. He had a remarkable career as a teacher of management at Notre Dame and encouraged my first extended use of slides.

For the Bicentennial in 1976, I had assembled a slide presentation, "American Literary Radicals and the Bicentennial, 1776-1976," for courses in American studies, at conferences, and on the church basement circuit. In time, that presentation evolved into "The American Tradition of Nonviolence, Thomas Paine to Martin Luther King," which I have given probably three hundred times, on every continent but Africa and Antarctica. In retrospect, the "evolution" seemed all of a piece. My many highways and byways and roundabouts, nonetheless, remind me of Robert Frost's description of a poet as someone whose random education sticks to him like cockleburs as he walks across a field.

Obviously, Mary Pat made much of that possible, while caring for six children, editing almost everything I wrote for publication, while completing a master's degree in psychology and responding to phone calls from people telling me, after an Op-Ed piece or a public lecture opposing the Vietnam war, to "Go back to Russia."

In 1979, another long anticipated, extraordinary opportunity came about: a grant from the American Philosophical Society to travel to Europe for the first time and to spend a month with Wilfred Owen's personal library housed at the English Faculty Library at Oxford and the British Museum in London.

ENGLAND AND WESTERN EUROPE

Here was history
As I desired it; magical, specific
Jumbled, unstinting

—Denise Levertov

Students were less likely in my 1950s college days to travel to Europe or Asia and Africa. Looking back, I realize that not doing so indicated a considerable lack of imagination on my part. Having read, studied, and taught English literature for years, I was obviously over prepared, at forty-five, to make the most of my first trip abroad. And I did.

From the moment of my arrival in London, the country seemed to respond generously to my long anticipated pilgrimage. My American Philosophical Society grant funded my research on Wilfred Owen, one of my favorite poets, and enabled me to visit literary landmarks and old friends both English and American. In London, I walked through Russell Square toward Bloomsbury Square, where small blue circles identified former residences of Leslie Stephen and Virginia Woolf and the birthplace of John Henry Newman. I went on to the British Museum, amid Egyptian exhibits, displays of Keats's letters, and other treasures. Even an inexpensive evening meal with red wine at the Spaghetti House in Gouge Street struck me as rather exotic.

Since my main destination was Oxford, the following day I took the train from Paddington Station and walked from the Oxford station to Campion Hall, the Jesuit residence, where an American Jesuit had arranged for me to stay. The location—just down the street from Corpus Christi College, around the corner from St. Aldate Church in one direction and the Newman Chapel and bookstores in the other—was, to me, the center of civilization. The daily routine at Campion of afternoon tea and a similar gathering after supper in the Common Room were equally civilized, even if residents appeared reluctant to engage American visitors. On an early morning walk across campus to the English Faculty Library, where Wilfred Owen's library was housed, I seldom made it past St. Aldate's coffee shop, before continuing down the High, past the Radcliffe Camera and New College to my final destination. My alternate route involved a short detour to the Magdalen Bridge or to Blackwell's bookstore, a sweet shop or pub along the way.

Following a full day in London and too many glasses of wine, I barely made the change at Didcot station on the return to Oxford. From the Oxford station I wobbled several blocks to Campion Hall just in time to lecture one of my hosts, an expert on liturgy, on what must be done to remedy the deteriorating condition of the institutional church. The next morning, fortunately, I left without having to face him again.

By that time, my Newman pilgrimage had already taken me to Trinity, his undergraduate college, to see the bust of him in the garden, and the Church of St. Mary the Virgin, where his lectures attracted large crowds, including Matthew Arnold and eminent Victorians. From there, it was only a short bus to Littlemore, where Newman decided to resign his fellowship before leaving the Anglican community and where Father Dominic Barberi received him into the Church of Rome. Since I had been an active member of Newman centers at universities in Oklahoma and Minnesota, especially after my meeting George Garrelts, Newman already occupied a significant place in my life. Mary Pat and I met at a seminar on Gerard Manley Hopkins at the Newman Center in Minneapolis, and our first son, Michael Newman, is named for him.

After Oxford, I went to Birmingham to visit Brian Wicker, a professor at University of Birmingham, as well as the Oratory, where Newman's library of ten thousand volumes is housed. In a room on the second floor, in the early 1860s, he sat at a small desk composing *Apologia Pro Vita Sua*, sometimes writing twenty hours a day. Later, approaching ninety, he continued to say mass in the same room, with mementos of his many friends, including the prime minister, attached to the wall above the altar. The Birmingham Oratory resonates with Newman's presence, in a way that Brompton Oratory in London, the residence of his troublesome fellow Oratorian, Father Frederic Faber, does not. Newman's books, *On the Development of Christian Doctrine,* 1845, and *Grammar of Assent,* 1870, as well as studies of the early Church Fathers, helped to bring the Catholic Church into the modern world. Conservative politically, yet progressive theologically, and spiritual father of the Second Vatican Council, Newman remains controversial a century after his death, with recent popes delaying his canonization.

Returning to London and the British Museum, when the library was still harbored there, I sat at a table in the reading room after requesting the poems of Wilfred Owen. When the librarian placed a large leather-bound book in my hands, I was surprised to discover that it included original manuscripts, many in Owen's handwriting. Some of them, written in the trenches in northern France during World War I, were blotted by raindrops. In amazement, tears on my cheeks, I sat in silence reading the poems that I had admired and taught for many years. A few days later, a friend and I drove through Oxfordshire, along the Thames, to a parsonage near Pangborne, where Owen resided before leaving for the Western Front. He was killed crossing a canal with his troops in November 1918, one week before the armistice.

While in London, Mary Richter, a friend and librarian at the American School, St. John's Wood, asked me to offer a writing workshop for secondary teachers there. That invitation turned out to be a blessing since it led to my repeating the workshop the following fall at the annual conference of the European Council of International Schools (ECIS). At those conferences I met some extraordinary teachers from international schools all over Europe, and spent time after the conferences on the continent.

Returning to London in November for that workshop enabled me to attend an international gathering of Pax Christi the following weekend, hosted by Victor Guazzelli, Bishop of East London. It included, along with presentations by well-known activists; a reception at the residence of Basil Hume, cardinal archbishop of London and my introduction to Tony Ives from Oxford; Valerie Flessati, head of Pax Christi; and Monsignor Bruce Kent. All was abuzz at Cardinal Hume's reception as he moved through the crowds shaking hands, the quick straight look, a civilized presence. Someone said that if the press could have elected a pope at the recent consistory, Cardinal Hume would have been the man, and one can see why. Handsome with a full head of gray hair and mildly ascetic, he knew who he was and what his responsibilities were, where they began and where they ended mildly. He spoke, in the words of Dylan Thomas, as if he had the Elgin Marbles in his mouth—naturally, forcefully, and intelligently about recent elections in Northern Ireland, the suffering of people in Indochina and Czechoslovakia. He endeared himself to me by quoting Newman.

Not long after that conference, Bruce Kent, following the historian E. P. Thompson, assumed the chairmanship of the Campaign for Nuclear Disarmament or CND. At the first event Bruce organized, ten thousand people showed up for a demonstration against nuclear weapons at Trafalgar Square. That movement eventually spread throughout western Europe, with millions of people involved, and led eventually to Gorbachev and Reagan signing a nuclear peace treaty in Iceland. At St. Antony's College, Oxford, Tony joined a number of academics in an effort to initiate a peace studies program, with initial presentations by a major military historian, Michael Howard, Regis Professor at Oxford, that led to further development later on.

At the conclusion of the Pax Christi conference, Valerie and Bruce invited me to join them at the home of Peggy Atlee, an inlaw of the former prime minister, near Keats's cottage in Hampstead. Later Tony Ives, associated with the Society of Friends in Oxford, introduced me to Charney Manor, a Quaker retreat center south of Oxford that proved to be consequential for my religious life.

From 1981 to 1983, I led workshops in writing and American literature at annual ECIS conferences, the stipend enabling me to see the sights in and around the Hague, Brussels, and Geneva. Thrilled to be touring Amsterdam, Paris, Florence, Venice, and Rome at long last, I felt like the legendary Okie who sunburned his tonsils ogling skyscrapers in Manhattan. Even the train rides between cities were exciting, particularly the one from Geneva through the Alps by Lake Como, arriving late at night in Venice and taking the vaporetto to St. Mark's Plaza and my night's lodging. Rome was equally thrilling no matter how often I had seen pictures or films of it. In contrast, an American standing beside me at the Fountain of Trevi announced to those gathered that he was quite disappointed in it. Fortunately, I didn't respond as I was inclined to do.

On a later visit, Mary Pat and I caught a glimpse of the pope from St. Peter's Square amid four hundred thousand other people. After dinner at a restaurant on the banks of the Tiber, I was drawn into a scene from Barber of Seville and "shaved" by the performing artist, to the amusement of our fellow tourists. When I suggested to one Boston tourist that he arrange an audience for us with Cardinal Bernard Law at Santa Maria Maggiore, he said that he would if he had a gun. Even after pedophile scandals, I never expected to hear such animosity toward the clergy from a Boston Irish Catholic.

Sights in Florence thrilled me even more than I expected, particularly *David*, "the most famous naked man in the world" at the Academia and the Piazza della Signoria across from Cellini's *Perseus* near the Uffizi and Palazzo Vecchio. As many times as I had seen copies of Botticelli's *Primavera*, nothing prepared me for the large canvas's brilliant gossamer light and subtle coloring. The other *David*, at the Michelangelo Piazzale overlooking the city, is not as beautiful as the original, but the elevated setting makes up for it with the Arno River below as well as the majestic duomo and Giotto's baptistery. Locally, *David* was regarded as "a mascot for a self-consciously democratic town surrounded by big bully city states."

In France, after a writing workshop at the American School at St. Germain-en-Laye, I spent several days walking around Paris, especially along the Left Bank. After visiting Sylvia Beach's Bookshop, resonant with meaning for any admirer of Hemingway and writers of the lost generation, dazzled by scenes around each corner and aware of my good fortune in being there, I crossed the Seine River Bridge on the way to Notre Dame Cathedral.

Years later, an international conference of anarcho-pacifists and former Communists took me to Grenoble, a stunning city along the river at the foot of the French Alps. By chance my visit coincided with a student-worker strike throughout the country. A First Employment Contract imposed by the prime minister had made it easier to lay off young people, without cause, during the first two years. Caught up in a demonstration in Grenoble, I overheard an elderly worker say at the time, "In France, we often think of companies, especially, as places of constant conflict between employees and management." Since the latter group lives "beyond the fault lines of left and right, companies," he continued, "and the market cannot be trusted." Within a week, the movement had successfully re-gained rights for workers and students, dramatizing the advantages of rights won by socialists in Europe that American workers might envy.

Although familiar with French socialist and anarchist traditions, in writing about the early twentieth century, I had never been among activists whose lives and careers were shaped by that history. A veteran of the French war in Algeria in the 1950s gave a history of that conflict, while others told moving stories about struggles for human rights, social justice and economic recovery. A Nigerian native explained that although a Christian pacifist movement exists there, it is overwhelmed by unrestrained violence among Muslim extremists in the north and paramilitaries in the south employed by Euro-American multinationals in the southern oil-rich Delta. An elderly Communist and former draft resister spoke of being hidden during the Algerian war by actors Yves Montand and Simone Signoret. The streets of Grenoble, named for Jean-Jacques Rousseau and Jean Juarez, as well as the Maison Stendahl, birthplace of the great novelist, gave resonance to both the conference and my walking tours. Quai Mounier, a bridge across the Isère River, remembers another native son, Emmanuel Mounier, pacifist, socialist, and editor of *L'Esprit,* who influenced the Second Vatican Council and was admired by Peter Maurin and Dorothy Day.

The encounters brought European history to life in a special way and led to my seizing unexpected opportunities for similar pilgrimages to East

Asia and, eventually, India. My time in Britain over a thirty year period deepened my affection for all things English. Members of the True family had left the Manchester area for Massachusetts in the mid seventeenth century, although my affection probably had more to do with geography, including the architecture and ambiance of London, Oxford, Durham, and Charney Manor.

A hopeless Anglophile, on return trips to Europe, I stopped in London where I stayed at the Penn Club near Russell Square and around the corner from Faber and Faber, the publishing house that employed T. S. Eliot. Walks in the city inevitably drew me to Tottenham Court Road to bookshops and the British Museum, particularly portraits of the First World War poets, whom I love. At Trafalgar Square, I boarded Bus 14, passing by Parliament and Westminster Abbey to Victoria Station and Westminster Cathedral, the rather Byzantine red and white marble structure about a mile from the abbey. My main purpose was to see Eric Gill's marvelous Stations of the Cross, but fortunately I arrived in time for a London Symphony Orchestra choral performance of Edward Elgar's *Dream of Gerontius* with a text by Cardinal Newman. In that area, each neighborhood offered numerous opportunities for living history, especially the Tate Museum and Buckingham Palace.

Thirteenth-century Charney Manor, a Society of Friends conference center, became a place of pilgrimage after 1979. Arriving at Heathrow, I took a bus and then a train to Reading and Didcot, traveling north through picturesque villages and winding hedgerows, near the Vale of the White Horse, to Charney Bassett, Oxfordshire. The Manor House had once belonged to a great Abingdon monastery before it was plundered by Henry VIII. A stone wall "contains" the garden at the back of the retreat center, its front and back entrances smothered in hawthorn and wisteria in bloom. From an upstairs window, one looks toward a stone bridge, an occasional rider on horseback passing over, and a pub only two blocks away.

After an annual conference of the International Peace Research Association in Groningen, the Netherlands, my wife and I made our way back to England again. Following several days at the Hague, among exhibits of paintings by Rembrandt, Vermeer, Rubens, and Brueghel, before going on to Delft, the Hook of Holland, we then crossed the North Sea to Delft. Our destination on that trip was Durham, where we spent a week in the university dorm, in the shadow of magnificent Durham Cathedral, with breakfast in the Palace's great hall and delicious scones and tea at the Almshouse. In the cool evenings, beneath the blue-gray sky and shadow of the silent cathedral, people strolled up the footpath from the river bridge and along the palace green. They were middle-class and elderly, husbands and wives, young couples with children, widows with daughters in short skirts, and punk rock young'uns with pink or orange hair and leather belts. Amid the abundant flower beds and beneath the spires and thick tower of St. Cuthbert, empire asserted itself in war memorials and heraldry from centuries before. Almost inevitably, I felt myself wondering how many of my ancestors from the region died hoisting heavy stones on stone for their daily bread in building those great monuments.

After a drive to Newcastle-on-Tyne, a train trip to Edinburgh, and an afternoon walking through the university environs and then toward Holyrood Palace and the Castle, we returned to the south of England to attend a retreat at Charney Manor. Led by Jim Pym, combining his deep knowledge of Buddhism and long involvement with Quaker faith and practice, it was the beginning of my renewed focus on religion, supplemented by recent scholarship of Diana Eck, John Dominic Crossan, and Karen Armstrong, among others. "In stillness, we go beyond the not-self, to the real self," Jim Pym had said, "toward nothingness, which is actually all." Years before, I might not have even heard or simply dismissed such reflections. But by my late fifties I was ready for them, and on returning home, I began attending Worcester Friends meetings and five years later presented myself for membership.

Later retreats at Charney and additional reading, meanwhile, helped me to understand and in a sense to reclaim positive aspects of my religious experience. On one occasion, Sheila Elworthy of the Oxford Research Group and author of *Power and Sex*, surrounded by candles, flowers, goddesses, and other symbols at Charney, emphasized the interconnectedness of body, mind, and spirit. Telling her about how much I had learned teaching and writing about nonviolence, she responded, "Even better is what you become." A journal entry at that time attempted to convey the effect of such encounters and of Charney itself over the years: "Is it real, this heaven on earth, with stretches of green, abundant flowers, bird song, gray clouds, and bright sun with an Eric Gill sculpture of Christ on a donkey just inside the entryway?"

In a letter to a friend that summer, I wrote, "so much has happened in a short time, all of it important." It was a reference to my sensing at Charney Manor a way of finding a path toward renewed religious faith, reconciling my Catholic identity, so elemental, and the Friendly Persuasion—the Society of Friends, the Quakers. "My goodness," I wrote in that letter, "isn't life a remarkable pilgrimage, a frequent setting out in a leaky boat. Fortunately, there are a few assurances, such as your friendship."

An entry in my journal about that time, mentions another important realization. "I had a sudden, unmistakable sense that my life as a writer is really beginning."

As a writer, I had long admired George Orwell, particularly *Homage to Catalonia* and his essays, including "Why I Write" in which he describes his working aesthetic. The verbal pyrotechnics of James Joyce, much admired by my colleagues, struck me as "mere rhetoric," while the simplicity of Orwell, it seemed to me, "grated on universal bones," as Faulkner said in his Nobel Prize speech. The plainness of Christopher Isherwood's prose also attracted me, his novels, as well as his memoir, *Christopher and His Kind*, which— not realizing how shocking his gay manifesto would be for some of them—I had assigned for my 1930s class. Unlike many writers, however, I had been slow in discovering my need to find language on the page and slower still to develop skills essential to writing well.

In a poem written about that time, I tried to indicate a sense of my aesthetic:

MANIFESTO

i

I see no need
for artifice,
for tricks or garnish.
The simple truth is poetic beyond measure.

ii

Among trees,
I prefer
the clarity of scrub oak
to the extravagance of maple, heavy
with metaphor and meaning.

iii

The baroque stands out,
but only in contrast to
the voluptousness
of what is plain, plain.

Cautiously and nervously submitting poems for publication, sometimes successfully, I found few editors interested in them, although a lyric for my brother and sister-in-law, celebrating their forty years of marriage, evoked positive response:

ANNIVERSARY
for Betty Ann and Herb

Daily, we say,
in spite of the ache of it,
"I marry you," choosing,
in the long journey out
of the self, uncertainty and
confusion over loneliness.
In a history of promises
kept or broke, we will
to make known the best
in us: gifts that heal

and comfort
like touches in the dark.
By day, we live the common
tasks-work, children,
debts, the evening meal.
At night, turning into or
away from one another,
we dream, then, our separate
worlds, constellations
of memory and desire,
reclaiming thus our
separate selves.
Each morning,
faithful as daylight
at the foot of the bed,
I marry you.

By the late seventies, my essays and reviews were appearing in *Commonweal, America, New Republic, The Progressive*, and other periodicals in the US and abroad. Having never attempted fiction, I ended up as a kind of pamphleteer after teaching argumentative writing for years and being seduced by writers such as Thomas Paine and Paul Goodman. Along the way, John Updike's take on what goes into writing offered a kind of encouragement.

There's a kind of confessional impulse that not every literate intelligent person has. A crazy belief that you have some exciting news about being alive, and I guess, that more than talent is what separates those who do it from those who think they'd like to do it.

> Writers often complain that they have no choice other than to do what they do. They "have to write." Such obstinacy is a bad habit and common failure among smokers, drinkers and television addicts as well.

Whenever I think of my time in England, I inevitably remember my dear friend Adam Curle, whom I met after reading his *Tools for Transformation: A Personal Study,* 1988, a gift from a longtime friend and peace activist, Frances Crowe. Among many other insights in the book are his reflections on organized religion, in the introduction, developed in a later section, "Who Am I," on the ego.

After reading the book and phoning him the next time I was in London, he generously came to meet me at the Penn Club, even though it was some distance from where he and Ann lived. Later, they invited Mary Pat and me to dinner when he insisted on traveling into Central London to accompany us, via Euston and Victoria Stations, across Vauxhall Bridge to East Dulwich, because of his concern for our safe passage through an antiwar demonstration. Well-known as the founder of the peace and conflict studies program at Bradford University, once the largest program in the world, he spoke modestly about his remarkable career mediating conflicts in dangerous areas, during the Biafran war, the civil war in Sri Lanka between Tamils and Singhalese, as well as in Zimbabwe, South Africa, Pakistan, India, and Northern Ireland. In his eighties, he accepted an invitation from a small community in Bosnia, the Osijek Centre, to help its members build a peace culture in that war-torn country.

Adam's intelligence and simplicity—his skills as a mediator—won him many admirers as a clinician, professor, and peacemaker since his techniques of peacemaking were an integrated whole, involving mediation, problem solving, negotiation, advocacy, and nonviolent direct action. And descriptions of those interventions suggest his calm and attentive manner, as he moved among warring governments and rebels to bring even recalcitrant rebels and diplomats together, when everyone else had failed. His personal and professional manner is suggested by the remark of a "dangerous adversary" after they had talked for an hour: "You are the first negotiator who ever smiled at me."

What endeared him to me was his presence, in the full sense of that word, resembling my earlier encounters with Dorothy Day, reflections by Desmond Tutu or the Dalai Lama, or poems by Walt Whitman. In each case, the person struck me as a force shaped by moral goodness, yet deeply human, conveying a hint of transcendence, one of those moments when, as Wilfred Cantwell Smith says, eternity intersects at right angles with everyday life. I am reminded of it each time I reread his last letter to me when, at ninety, he continued writing his effort to make clear his "concept of this universe." In the meantime, he concluded, "let me say how much your friendship has meant to me and that I send to you and your dear wife the warmest and most loving greetings."

Traveling in England and western Europe after 1979, particularly my personal encounters there, furthered my experience and appreciation for matters related to literature and culture. It ultimately had a profound effect on my religious life as well.

CHINA AND KOREA

The Yangtze River
which Jimmy and I named long ago
in geography games after school.

—"Yangtze"

Traveling in Europe and teaching at writers conferences in Minnesota and Arkansas as well as publishing a book and various essays led to an unexpected adventure. Through Zhang Ziqing, a scholar at the Foreign Language Research Institute at Nanjing University (Nanda) in 1984, I was invited by the Education Department in China to spend a year teaching American literature to graduate students and undergraduates. Somewhat to my surprise, since our children were by that time all in college, Mary Pat agreed that we should accept the offer to be there a full year.

I had met Zhang Ziqing, a fellow at Harvard's Yinching Institute, almost by accident, after a colleague at Worcester State College asked me if I would be willing to talk with him about contemporary poetry. At our last meeting, when he mentioned me coming to China, I agreed that it was a nice idea, never expecting that anything would come of it. Several months later, a letter of invitation arrived saying, in characteristic Chinese fashion, that if I accepted the invitation, I was invited, but if I didn't accept it, I wasn't invited.

No one was more surprised than I to find myself landing at the Shanghai airport in August 1984. On our arrival, the only airplane on the runway, my wife and I walked down the stairway toward a one-story, dilapidated terminal building with a single, low-watt light bulb over the entrance. After twelve hours in an air-conditioned plane, eighty-seven-degree heat felt like a hundred and ten. Under instructions from a young

95

English instructor from Nanjing University, uniformed customs officials moved us quickly through the routine check-in, as an ai- conditioned cab awaited us in the parking lot. The driver whisked us along dark streets, our headlights flashing on and off to save the battery as people on bicycles or on foot, including lovers holding hands, scurried out of the way.

After a long drive across Shanghai to the far side of the city, we arrived at a physical education college for lodging that night. Crumbling tiled bathroom floors, a poorly constructed building with windows askew and hard beds were something of a shock. So was the food, including something pickled for breakfast. In the afternoon, we boarded the train for the two-hundred-mile ride west to Nanjing. In lush green fields, with water buffalo along canals in the distance, men and women worked the fields of rice and rapeseed with hand tools and moved among stucco buildings grouped around a courtyard.

Jiangsu Province, with a population of sixty million people, is famous for agricultural and industrial production, while Nanjing, its capital of three million people, is known as one of "the furnace cities" along with Wuhan and Chongqing further along the Yangtze River. A sophisticated city of historic sites, museums, and well-known universities, it competed with Beijing as the national capital during various dynasties and served as Chiang Kai-Shek's headquarters before the Japanese war. An impressive memorial to national hero Sun Yat-sen, on the outskirts of the city, attracts many foreign tourists and entrepreneurs. Asian and Eastern Europeans come to the city to study geology and astronomy at Zijin, or Purpose, Mountain observatory overlooking the city. As China extended its reach beyond Asia, African male students came to study engineering, dating Chinese women and my colleagues from abroad. In time, however, Chinese prejudice against black people asserted itself and led to bad feeling and campus riots against them.

On our arrival in an air-conditioned train at the station, Mary Pat nearly fainted from the heat. Along the ride from there to the campus, we saw people moving cots from their apartments onto the sidewalk, to find relief from the heat. The three-story Foreign Experts Building on campus,

Nanjing colleagues

our home for the coming year, was adequate, even luxurious by local standards, with one air-conditioned room in summer and occasional heat in winter. In winter, when foreign teachers complained about thirty degree classrooms, we were informed that China, for no apparent reason, "does not heat south of the Yangtze River." With chilblains on their hand and cheeks, both teachers and students huddled in winter coats, as cold air poured in through broken windows.

Before leaving the US, I had begged twenty-five copies of literature texts for graduate students over the next year and anthologies on argumentative writing, since few copies of books in English were available in China. Some of them arrived from the US slightly ahead of us, but others, which a vigilant colleague discovered almost by accident, ended up in a heap in the corner of a post office nearby. One afternoon, after loading them in a pedicab, the driver and I sailed downhill on Zhongshan Lu at about forty miles an hour. Fortunately, no pedestrian, bicycle, tractor or automobile blocked our path or we would have ended up a heap along the roadside.

Once classes began, I enjoyed meeting students and faculty, thinking my way through various approaches to teaching writing and literature. Mary Pat, a school psychologist and former editor, taught English writing to first-year students, several of them curious about her psychology books, which eventually made their way around campus. Soon, the weiban, the Foreign Affairs Office—formerly known as the Office of Barbarian Affairs—scheduled events for us, including occasional banquets, a Chinese opera, art exhibits and trips to historic sites.

Living on campus, we often met foreign visitors, including well known English academics and artists, including E. P. and Dorothy Thompson and A. S. Byatt, from England, members of the American Council of Learned Societies, and other dignitaries from abroad who stayed in our building. Felicity Breet, a skilled language teacher with the British Council, and I gave poetry readings that attracted large audiences curious about twentieth-century American and British literature. My close friend, Zhang Ziqing, whom I met in Massachusetts, proved to be an exceptional host who introduced us to local artists, poets, army officers and dignitaries, including master calligraphers and painters at the Nanjing College of Art. A truly remarkable person, he also arranged for a chef from Suzhou, known for its exceptional cuisine, to prepare an unforgettable banquet for our benefit and accompany me to speak at colleges and university, where Mary Pat and I were inevitably treated with courtesy and generosity.

Since he was translating poems by T. S. Eliot and contemporary poets into Chinese, Zhang Ziqing and I worked together closely, publishing essays and books. Working with him, I learned as much as he did about T. S. Eliot's *The Wasteland* and numerous poems by contemporary American writers. "As busy as bees," in his words, he was constantly outlining projects for us, such as essays on the relationship between Chinese and American literature, which appeared as an anthology in Chinese. He also translated my introduction to his translations of Eliot and brief commentaries on contemporary poets.

With his wife, two daughters, and his mother-in-law, Zhang Ziqing lived in a fifth-floor walk-up, in a drab concrete building near campus. In winter, at a desk in his small apartment, he was unable to hold a writing pen because his fingers were too cold. Indefatigable, persistent, and industrious through it all, he is regarded as a national literary figure who corresponds with artists and scholars around the world. After our time together in China, on fellowship a second time in the US, he became friendly with a number of American writers, including Allen Ginsberg.

Most of the eight thousand undergraduate and graduate students at Nanda had studied English at some point, as well as other European languages, and I found their facility with language impressive. Several of the twenty-four—workers, soldiers, peasants during the Cultural Revolution—learned English at considerable risk to themselves, listening to the BBC late at night after working all day in the fields.

China had been open to Americans for only about three years, and many men and women still wore Mao jackets. Professors at the university, among the best known academics in China, lived on monthly salaries amounting to about a tenth of mine during my residency. My colleague, Wu Keming, lived with his wife and daughter in one room with a cold shower at the end of the hall and shared a kitchen with five other families in a building that must have barely survived the Japanese war. Generous and hospitable when they invited us to their home, his wife spent her only day off shopping for food in stores where many of the shelves were empty before preparing seven or eight dishes for the evening meal. Several distinguished faculty members had been exiled to the countryside or imprisoned in basements of campus buildings during the Cultural Revolution. Most of those policies were already beginning to change by 1984 and within ten years people's lives attained a standard that one could hardly dream of during our time there.

From the courtyard outside the Foreign Experts Building we heard the sounds of the city, as pedestrians, bicycles, a few cars, and heavy trucks filled the crowded streets in the early morning just beyond the university wall. Blaring from speakers around campus, the national anthem awakened us every morning with songs such as "Waltzing Matilda" playing over and over throughout the day. Our meals were served cafeteria-style in a nearby dining hall where daily fare included burnt toast ("ashtrays," my son called them), coffee, and edible food except for roasted chicken at supper with heads and feet attached. Someone had told the chef that Americans preferred their cooking with heavy oil, so in emergencies, yogurt provided adequate nourishment.

Students lived eight to a room and in winter took to their bunks and thick, heavy blankets to keep warm. In thirty-degree classrooms, with cold wind blowing through the windows, everyone wore coats, scarves, and hats. Unlike several of my students, however, I never had chilblains on my ears, cheeks, and hands. Although the university library had literary reference works, librarians behaved more as "bookkeepers" than helpful attendants. Note or typing paper of any kind was scarce, and crossing the campus exposed everyone to coal dust belched from the central heating plant. Along hallways, odors from the bathroom were strong enough to knock your hat off.

The inconveniences were manageable, however, and my students were genuinely interested in American literature and culture, including the Puritans, "the first revolutionaries." Initially, they told me that serious students at the university studied English writers and read American novels for fun, so I assumed they read more American than English literature. Although courteous and disciplined, they struck me as a bit grim, observing me closely and objectively for the first few weeks. When they appeared skeptical about the course syllabus in American literature, I told them that we could approach the reading any way—forwards, backwards, sideways, or circling around. Fortunately, they decided my plan to proceed chronologically made sense. Telling them that they could learn a lot from me if they chose to, I counseled them to speak to me directly, rather than behind my back, a tactic students used in distancing themselves from foreign teachers. After that discussion, we never had any trouble.

In time, they took a liking to novels by Willa Cather, John Steinbeck, and J. D. Salinger, especially, and to modern poetry, particularly Robert Frost and William Carlos Williams. All twenty-four of them learned to write English with extraordinary competence by the end of our year together, with all but one of them choosing to write theses on American literature. Several eventually completed graduate degrees at major universities in the US and teach at prep schools, colleges, and major universities in the US as well as China.

For many years, only one in a thousand Chinese went to university, and the students had jumped through many hoops to get there. Entrance examinations were highly competitive. At my office for a tutorial, one of the students commented that she had been the outstanding student in English. Complimenting her, I asked if that meant that she was the outstanding student in English at Nanda. "No," she replied, lowering her head, "in China." Admission to a university assured a person of a rice bowl for life, whether iron, gold or silver. Although undergraduates were as intelligent as graduate students, they did not feel the impetus to study hard once they got there, occasionally transferring to universities principally in the US, England, and Australia.

In October 1984 on the thirty-fifth anniversary of the 1949 revolution, we boarded a boat on the great Yangtze River for an overnight trip to Nantong. Numerous ships of all sizes and descriptions traveled to and fro under the long bridge that spanned the river, on their way to Wuxi and Shanghai. Odors in the passageway testified to the long voyage from Wuhan. Traveling fourth class, I stayed awake, watching through the window below my upper bunk as small carriers, barges, and large ships moved, as we moved, along the straits and into the heart of the current. In the night, I woke to rain on the deck, the heavy change on the dark misty river. Used to being surrounded by land on all sides, I longed for some assurance of safety.

The next morning, a woman's voice roused us, followed by a recording of the national anthem, classical Chinese music, and Chopin, which added to the romance of the river. After festivities in Nantong, as the oldest guest—or at least the one with the grayest hair, I sat beside the captain of a Russian vessel in the harbor for a banquet celebration. We headed west again. In Zhenjiang, after heavy rain on the river, the skies cleared, and the sun came out. We saw lush farms, wide inlets, and canals along the river and in green hills with pagodas and shrines near the top of them in the distance. Unexpectedly, below deep gouges in the hillside, the river bank turned industrial, with flat cars of gravel and sand on their way to construction sites. At noon, the boat pulled under the long bridge across the Yangtze and into the dock. A bus then took us along the tree-lined streets and into the heart of the city. As a child, my friend Jimmy Ralph and I had named the Yangtze River in geography games after school. Once I had been there, actually traveled that river, it was no more real to me, though mightier, more essential, and mysterious than before.

During Christmas vacation, my wife and I flew in a rickety Russian plane to Xian to see the magnificent terra cotta warriors and carriages, where excavators continued to liberate rows on rows of buried treasure. Although the museums and warriors, as well as the wall around the city are impressive, frigid weather up north surprised us, and the heavy drapes over the circular doorways were little protection from the cold. On the train ride back to Nanjing, we bundled head-to-toe, but my nose remained icy cold.

Traveling by train, a safer bet than the Russian airplane, and arriving in Nanjing on Christmas Eve, we attended midnight mass at the old cathedral. Numerous television camera crews broadcast the festivities, which attracted large crowds inside and outside the cathedral. On entering, and somewhat to our embarrassment, Mary Pat and I were immediately ushered up front, after ushers quickly cleared out a front pew for foreign guests. Amid the excitement and bright lights, my wife failed to recover her scarf and gloves, which disappeared when we went up to the altar rail to receive communion. This bishop and congregation were associated with the "official" Chinese Catholic church, as were the cathedrals in Shanghai and Guangzhou, at that time separated from the Vatican.

On a later holiday, we took the nine-hundred mile train ride north to Beijing, with an opportunity to visit ancient Ming tombs and the Great Wall beyond the city. The effect of walking along the mighty Wall reminded me of wading across the source of the mighty Mississippi, reduced to a small stream near Lake Itaska, Minnesota, years before.

During spring festival, we traveled south and then across the river to Hong Kong, after spending the night at a five star hotel in Guangzhou. Since neither our Chinese nor our foreign currency were any good in Hong Kong, we used a Visa card at the hotel and restaurants, then borrowed money from residents who befriended us at the Congregational Church.

Returning to Nanjing, we welcomed two of our children, Chris and Anne, who had just arrived from the US amid signs of spring. During the second semester, Chris and Anne, after studying intensive Chinese at the University of Massachusetts, taught English conversation to first year students at Nanda. In May, just before speaking at Suzhou University, I received a long distance phone call informing us that our first grandchild, Jonathan, had been born to John and his wife, Mary Julie, married the previous fall in Worcester.

In July, unable to leave China from Shanghai for some unexplainable reason, we took the train from Nanjing to Beijing, then flew back to Shanghai and on to Tokyo, New York and Boston. Before leaving Beijing, Mary Pat and I saw Chris and Anne off on the long Trans-Siberian Railway trip across Manchuria and Russia. After Poland and Germany, they parted company, Chris going to Italy and Anne to England. Once we were back in Worcester, frantic phone calls from Chris, at a parking lot in Florence, then Geneva and Paris, informed us that he was without any money. Luckily, he was able to hitchhike some of the time, to stay at someone's apartment in Switzerland and at a residence of the Assumption Sisters in Paris, where the American embassy gave him $25. The patience and generosity of friends enabled him and Anne eventually to enjoy Ireland for several days before flying home.

After time at home, I returned to teach for two months in 1987 at Nanjing Normal University, a provincial rather than a national university, like Nanda. The students, again, were very talented. Living in university quarters, I spent a good deal of time with them, happy to have two of them accompany me on a trip to Wuxi, a city of lakes and parks not far from Nanjing.

With a greater variety of vegetables and fruits along with eel, shrimp, and pork, available in the free market just outside the university gate, life appeared a bit easier for the Chinese than it must have been two years before. Farmers sold extra produce at similar markets, which meant greater prosperity for them, but has also led to inflation and created hardship for city workers, whose incomes had not as yet increased with rising prices. Eggs, for example, were twice as expensive as two years before. Construction sites promised better living conditions for city dwellers and privately owned stores and vendors were common throughout the city. Clothing, including multi-colored skirts, blouses and shirts were plentiful in shops, as were notebooks, dishes and toiletries.

Having visited a number of churches and met Chinese Christians during my previous year in China, I welcomed the opportunity that time to meet Bishop K. H. Ting, president of China Christian Council and head of Nanjing Theological Seminary. An alumnus of Union Theological Seminary in New York, he had been directly responsible for the flourishing spirit of Christianity in China, working closely with the Amity Foundation, which provides support from abroad in education, health and social services, as well as the publications of Bibles in Chinese. His recent address in Beijing, "Christian Sharing Across Nation Boundaries: As a Chinese Sees It," widely quoted, served somewhat as a global force bolstering transnational ambitions for those "inspired by national and corporate interests rather than the disinterested good will and generosity of Christians and their care for other people."

Since the Cultural Revolution, Bishop Ting has seen the re-opening of four thousand Protestant churches and the establishment of nine theological institutes, "though the leadership of both Catholic and Protestant churches is elderly, with a great need for extensive theological education." Responding to my question about recent disciplining of writers and intellectuals and student demonstrators, Bishop Ting emphasized that the principles of self-government, self-support and self-propagation must be honored by everyone. Saying that the Church in China is to be "governed by Chinese Christians and not by foreign missionaries," he indicated that China will have an increasing influence on the international Christian church, both Protestant and Catholic.

Returning to China in turmoil in 1989 as a guest of Nanjing University, I arrived in the midst of the democratic uprising, a classic nonviolent movement involving millions of people. Inspired and up to that point conducted by students from major universities in Beijing, it focused on several grievances. After ten years of limited economic reform, amid corruption and lack of freedom of the press, intellectuals and city dwellers, particularly, felt betrayed by the party and the government. Soon joined by increasing numbers of peasants and workers, they spoke out against Beijing's repressive policies, including extensive political re-education programs on campuses. Between April and the time of my arrival in Shanghai from Tokyo on May 17, protests had spread from Tiananmen Square to three hundred cities across the country. Media coverage centered on Beijing and through a sophisticated communication system drew together students, peasants, workers, and intellectuals, traditionally antagonistic toward one another.

My arrival coincided with the arrival of President Mikhail Gorbachev, the first major Russian official to visit China in thirty years. One of my former students made the long bicycle ride from the far side of the city to meet me and to accompany me to a campus near the center of the city. Demonstrations continued throughout the night just below the window of my dormitory at Shanghai Institute of Foreign Trade, and the next morning my cab to the railway station had to make a wide detour to avoid huge crowds at the center of the city.

1989 Nanjing protest

By the time I arrived in Nanjing it was in turmoil, with a hundred thousand demonstrators in the streets. Since the cab driver was reluctant to take me all the way to the university, I eventually made my way by pedicab, through side streets and small lanes. On campus, a huge, colorful banner covered a wall in the Foreign Experts Building. Its message "Youth and skill are no match for old age and treachery," resembled other hand-lettered posters covering student bulletin boards at the university gate. Local university students had already initiated a Long March to Beijing to join their contemporaries as others took to the streets throughout the country.

Supplicant, initially, student protesters cared enough about their country to call their elders to account on matters that affected everyone—censorship, nepotism and corruption. For many Chinese the uprising resonated with the May 4 Movement, 1919, when an earlier generation of students called their elders to account and in a movement that led to the birth of modern China. This time, they made every effort not to isolate themselves from workers and townspeople, who regard them as an elite, which, of course, they are. Older people recognized, nonetheless, that students reflected their own dissatisfaction with the party's Central Committee of old men who had lost touch with a younger generation.

In Beijing, students from major universities in Beijing occupied Tiananmen Square, where some of them began a fast, refusing water until foreign journalists warned them against doing so. In a movement that was basically nationalistic, student leaders knelt before government officials at the edge of the huge square, with long, signed petitions advocating freedom of the press. Disregarded and told to disperse, the disciplined crowd became more militant, even defiant, knowing that even some party members supported them.

Each morning in Nanjing, students gathered at the university gate and walked to historic Gu Lou Square for a day-long assembly, to be joined by others for speeches and protests. Along the sidewalks, people applauded students, who formed a cordon around the demonstrators to prevent anyone from disrupting their purposeful march. Standing on the sidelines so as not to be accused of being an "outside agitator," I was deeply impressed by the young people's sophistication in conducting a nonviolent movement, though apprehensive at the same time about what might happen to them.

Loudspeakers on the Nanda campus broadcast "The Internationale" and the national anthem repeatedly as Nanda students maintained constant and direct communication by phone, internet, and fax machine with compatriots throughout the country. Campus posters and banners quoted the nineteenth-century Englishman Lord Acton on the corruptive influence of power and Dr. King on dreams of freedom. A recent poem by Bei Dao echoed the defiant mood of the demonstrators:

Wickedness is the passport of the wicked . . .
Look, floating in the sky
are the tortured shadows of the dead . . .
Being sentenced, I will speak my piece
I shall say to the world, I accuse!
And although you trod a thousand resisters underfoot,
I shall be the one thousand and first.

Many faculty joined the student protests, expressing their impatience with party leadership under Deng Xiaoping and Li Peng. An academic vice-president and party member gave the strongest speeches I heard supporting the movement. Within a week, faculty, discouraged by the government's response to student petitions, sensed its developing hard line. During a dinner for me on campus, the expressions on the faces of faculty reflected their deep concern, though no one that I knew, Chinese or foreigner, expected the massacre two weeks later.

In late May, Zhang Zing, a graduate student, and I took the train fifteen hundred miles north to Harbin to participate in an international conference on American literature at Heilongjang University. Although crowds filled the street there as well, the conference proceeded without incident. On the second day, I joined friends for dinner downtown at a Russian restaurant. The city's architecture and customs reflected the fact that thousands of White Russians had sought refuge in the region in 1917. The Japanese had occupied the city until they were defeated in World War II.

On the morning of June 4, arriving for breakfast, a Chinese scholar from East China Normal University stood at the foot of the stairs, tears running down his cheeks. Since expressions of emotion are rare among Chinese, I feared the worst. The father of college-age children in Beijing, he had just learned from BBC and Voice of America that government troops had fired into crowds in Tiananmen Square. Observers noted that the soldiers were from remote regions of the country, perhaps taking revenge on Han people, whose dominance they resented and whose language they barely understood. As workers and others swelled the angry crowds, the country's ruling party panicked. The brutal crackdown ended in tragedy, particularly for workers. Some estimates indicated that approximately three hundred students and as many as two thousand workers died when soldiers in tanks and armored cars moved against unarmed demonstrators in Beijing.

Still in Harbin, the mood turned angry when residents learned that four students from its University of Science and Technology were among those who were killed at Tiananmen Square. Wall posters pictured Li Peng and his compatriots as Nazis wearing swastikas, in bloody-red Chinese characters. Tension in Harbin increased, with roadblocks at major intersections.

After the conference ended, going to the station to board a train back to Nanjing, our cab was stopped twice at barricades before students let us pass. The journey went smoothly for the first thousand miles until the train reached Jili, in Shandong province about halfway to Nanjing. Rumors had it that the army was in revolt, but actually a fire on a train in Shanghai had halted traffic on the main route to and from Beijing.

After sitting in the Jilin train station for twelve hours, at Zhang Ziqing's suggestion, my friends and I ran across the tracks to board a local train. Leaving a comfortable sleeper, we boarded a car with hard, wooden seats to sit among workers and farmers as students fanned throughout the train to inform them about the uprising. Fifty hours after leaving Harbin, on a trip that usually took thirty-three hours, we arrived at Nanjing on the north side of the Yangtze River, took a ferry across and then a bus to the center of town. Local and university officials had wisely sent students home before the official end of the semester, so the streets were quiet, with a few soldiers in jeeps patrolling the streets. Most foreign teachers had already left the Foreign Experts Building on a special plane to Hong Kong provided by the Canadian embassy.

Within a few days, remnants of the movement had practically disappeared, and university bulletin boards were stripped of wall posters as the government began re-writing the history of the movement. Faculty obviously wanted to prevent students from further harm, knowing that any direct confrontation with the government was unwise, perhaps even suicidal. State propaganda claimed that no students had been killed in Beijing and praised soldiers for the valiant defense of the motherland against "rascals," "hoodlums" and "counter-revolutionary elements." My main worry was whether the government would move against the intellectuals, including my former students, as it had during the Cultural Revolution. Surprisingly, many participants, in contrast to earlier protests, found reasons to stonewall government officials in their effort to identify the troublemakers, although others were imprisoned and perhaps executed.

After martial law was imposed, wall posters and slogans became increasingly hostile toward Li Peng, who was petitioned to retract a denunciation of the movement and initiate reforms. Instead, television commentators confined themselves to reading government proclamations and highly censored accounts of events. Looking straight into the camera, they spoke in a tone of voice and expression implying that no viewer should take seriously what they said on camera.

In the meantime, after a phone conversation with one of the editors, I agreed to write articles about my time in China for my home newspaper. When a former student teaching at the Foreign Affairs Institute visited me, he delighted in telling about reading Thoreau's "Civil Disobedience" in his class. Worried about his getting into trouble with the authorities, I learned that, instead, he had been appointed to the Chinese embassy in India.

Having been told that Northwest Airlines had left China, I immediately tried to find another flight home. The train to Shanghai proved to be an unusual experience, with only three people in the passenger car, including a student who insisted on accompanying me to the airport, with a journalist from the British newspaper, The Independent. As I boarded the United flight home, an attendant asked me if I would be willing to look after a young girl who, because of turmoil in China, was being sent by her parents to San Francisco. When I agreed to do so, the stewardess whisked us both to the first class section.

Significant changes in China were obvious during the turmoil, particularly in Shanghai and Harbin. Luxury hotels were commonplace wherever I traveled, best represented perhaps by the new Shanghai airport so dramatically different from the clapboard, weather-beaten structure that welcomed Mary Pat and me five years earlier.

Two years later, I returned to Beijing on my way to North Korea and later received three invitations to teach at universities in Nanjing but I never got there. According to the consulate, my official papers never reached them, while a host university decided that it had no residence for foreign teachers though I had stayed there previously. The reason for the invitations being withdrawn according to China scholars in the US, was the publication of my essay, "The Democratic Uprising in China: A

Nonviolent Perspective," reprinted several times and listed on the internet for anyone who googled my name.

This minor incident coincided with the Chinese government's success in eradicating the uprising from history. It remains, nevertheless, in the words of China specialist Orville Schell, "one of the largest and best organized nonviolent political protest movement the world has ever seen." The students learned quickly as they went along, improvising and keeping alert in the face of overwhelming odds in an effort to uphold freedom of the press and to resist nepotism and corruption. And they deserve a very special place in the memories of anyone committed to the common good and to nonviolent social change. Although the Communist leadership denied that the uprising had ever happened and succeeded in erasing it from Chinese history, it contributed to the ongoing modernization of China.

To my surprise in 1991, returning to Beijing on my way to North Korea reminded me of previous difficulties in getting about. Leaving the international airport on my way to the hotel, the cabbie drove around in circles to increase my fare, although we finally compromised on the amount without much difficulty. And I eventually succeeded in obtaining a visa for North Korea and flying to Pyongyang.

The country gave me an eerie feeling from the moment our plane, the only one in sight, landed on the long runway in Pyongyang. Whisked about in a Mercedes with a driver and guide, we came into the city's concrete landscape of monuments and wide boulevards—a stark showplace with few people or cars on the street. Appearing industrious, disciplined and distant, everybody I saw wore small badges with a picture of the Great Leader, Kim Il-sung, over their hearts. Throughout the visit, I kept thinking of incidents in Korea's tragic history, particularly the cruel domination by Japan between 1915 and 1945, followed by the Korean War, when, according to Jon Halliday, "North Korea was more devastated than any country during World War." War crimes, in violation of international law, were committed by both sides in the still unresolved conflict between the US and North Korea.

As a guest of the Juche Institute, a government think tank headed by Hwang Jang-yap, a high-ranking member of the central committee of the

Workers' Party, I was treated cordially by him and his staff, who were attentive to my slide presentation on nonviolent movements in US history. Ironically, seven years later, Hwang Jang-yap escaped to the South Korean

North Korean colleagues and Michael, right, in Pyongyang

Embassy in Beijing, seeking political asylum before flying on to Seoul. On several occasions, according to a *New York Times* article in April, 2010, members of the North Korean secret service, disguised as defectors to the South, came very close to assassinating him.

The high point of my time in North Korea was a visit with English teachers at Kim Il-sung University, who were happy to learn about American writers whom they were not allowed to cover in their classes and to accept my handouts, mainly poetry fliers. My conversations with them made me long to return to teach there, which I tried to do on my return home; but nothing came of it. Every library we visited was filled to capacity, reflecting what I had heard about the high literacy rate in the country. Although resplendent with classical Korean paintings from the past, museums were dominated by recent socialist-realist canvases and sculptures. On a massive theater stage before a large audience, an elaborate perfectly synchronized troop of dancers, acrobats, and singers entertained us for two hours. And before I left the country, guides took me on a brief tour beyond the city to the Sea of Japan.

Returning to Beijing, I was told by Air China that my reservation to Tokyo had been canceled. Somewhat in a panic, since that endangered my connecting flight to Chicago, I went directly to the office of Air China several miles from the hotel and parked myself at the counter, determined to reclaim my ticket. Fortunately, after forty-five minutes, the attendant checked the seating assignments once again and informed me that he had found the "last ticket" on my flight. When I boarded the plan for Tokyo, however, it was less than half full.

My introduction to Korean culture on that trip led to my visiting South Korea ten years later. Although my previous knowledge of its tragic history was limited in spite of my living through the Korean War, Bruce Cumming's excellent two-volume history, *Origins of the Korean War,* provided essential background and history, quoting General Curtis LeMay's testimony before Congress that "over a period of three years or so, we burned down every town in North Korea—and South Korea too." Although the cruelties Koreans endured under the Japanese are well known, I was ignorant about the alliance between US occupation forces in 1945 and Koreans who collaborated with the Japanese, or the vicious destruction of the labor movement that followed. Even after two generations under repressive regimes allied with the US, Korean workers and students continue to challenge those in power. And I was deeply moved on entering Seoul's Catholic cathedral, which the cardinal archbishop opened as a sanctuary to nonviolent resisters escaping arrest and torture that awaited them in the 1970s.

Americans who took courageous stands against the Korean government at that time included Maryknoll Father Blasé Bonpane, who was deported for standing with those resisting oppression. Muriel Rukeyser, the American poet who was president of PEN at the time, stood in the rain for three days outside the prison gates near Seoul, where a well-known poet, Kim Chi Ha, was incarcerated, facing execution. His work, translated by Daniel Berrigan and Denise Levertov, had been published in the US as artists around the world came to his support. After Rukeyser's intervention, Kim was released. Being there made me curious about documentation of nonviolent campaigns over the centuries, during Korea's occupation by China, Japan, Russia, and, finally, the US.

In a burst of enthusiasm at the next International Peace Research Association conference, a young Indian scholar at Oxford and I planned a six-volume history on nonviolent movements on each continent, and Jae Bong Lee, a Korean scholar, and I arranged to work together on a history of similar movements in his native country. Although that ambitious project never materialized, unfortunately, the consequences of my going to East Asia, as well as Australia and New Zealand, altered my global perspective and contributed to my writing about nonviolent campaigns elsewhere in the world.

Little did I realize how much my time in Asia would influence my religious sensibility, until then narrowly Western and provincial. The effect of it was particularly apparent after teaching in India shortly afterward, which won my heart and mind in ways that I never expected. Having been told earlier that the Chinese weren't religious, I soon began to think that if they weren't religious, something was seriously wrong with one's definition of "religion." Further reading in the works of theologians and religious historians, including Han Kung and Karen Armstrong, confirmed my suspicions.

Over the next several years, I began to feel increasingly uncomfortable with liturgies associated with Western religions, Protestant or Catholic, which seemed equally exclusionary, as well as peculiarly bookish and distant. After Pope Paul VI and by 2000, institutional Catholicism had undergone a retrenchment, theologically and pastorally, which undermined hopes and promises associated with the Second Vatican Council. In a journal entry in 1989, I had faulted Catholicism for imposing "too much *should* on children."

It became clear to me also that Catholics, particularly in the Northeast, seldom questioned the authoritarian structure of the Church. Even as they criticized it or even left its embrace, they remained reluctant to explore other faiths. Even after my sixty years as an active Catholic, some of my former co-religionists treated me as if I no longer belonged to the club when I became interested in other religions.

Eventually, my familiarity with Quakers through my long association with and admiration for American Friends Service Committee offered the possibility of my regaining a positive context for religious practice. But it was several years after returning from China that I attended Friends meetings in 1990 and another five years before I came to think of myself as a very Catholic Quaker.

BACK HOME

Returning from China in July 1985, Mary Pat and I were happy to find cooler weather, or at least cooler than in China. In addition to a festive reunion with most of the family, for the first time we saw our beautiful grandchild, Jonathan Timothy True, and shortly afterward celebrated his baptism at Blessed Sacrament Church, Worcester.

My return to classes that fall went smoothly, though the campus was in turmoil, with faculty and administration engaged in a conflict over the future of the undergraduate curriculum. Although we had a strong core that gave students the illusion of choice, guiding them into areas of study appropriate for a liberal arts education, the administration was bent on forcing students to repeat surveys similar to their high school offerings. That restrictive program also acquired students for teachers who were less well educated and more parochial than others. After voting down the administration's curriculum seven times, the faculty eventually caved in to administrative pressure and manipulation. The resulting program seemed disastrous to me, particularly after my time in Asia.

Adopting a restrictive curriculum, in line with recommendations by Lynne Cheney and other bureaucrats opposed to global studies, the college required all students to study two semesters about so-called Western Civilization. Not surprisingly, when I asked students over the next few years how things were going, at least two thirds of them insisted they "hated history," not to mention the required courses in philosophy and theology. Although that curriculum proved unworkable, requiring changes almost every year, it hung on for a decade, contributing to the faculty's frustration. In time, it led to further conflicts during the administration of several super-Catholic administrators, supported by the Assumptionists and board of trustees.

Personal losses at that time also provoked significant changes and adjustments. My mother's death in 1986 along with my father's six years earlier made me feel as if there were no longer any barrier between me and the North Pole. Visiting her when she was ill had made me feel as if my connection with her was intact, but her death meant the loss of any intimate contact with Oklahoma. Fortunately, I sought the help of a counselor, a learned psychotherapist, who helped me to integrate body, mind and spirit and to make connections between my personal and public lives. Also, his extraordinary knowledge of religious traditions, with distinctive psychological implications, proved to be equally helpful.

Gradually, I came to appreciate parallels between the history of psychology in the nineteenth century and the history of peace, conflict, and nonviolence studies in the twentieth century. As relatively "new" disciplines committed to healing—the first of the individual psyche and the latter of the social order—both had faced opposition initially, since they challenged conventional wisdom about the nature of conflict. Peace studies, particularly, maintains that conflict is inevitable, but violence is not. The publication in 1986 of UNESCO's Statement on Violence, by internationally known psychologists, anthropologists and psychiatrists challenging the notion that human beings are innately violent, had a significant effect; but my education in the social sciences was random and halting, as I struggled to reinvent myself.

The following decade at Assumption proved to be engaging and even exciting, as a result of my commitment to peace and conflict studies, teaching at various colleges and universities, and trying to integrate my academic and activist interests. This led to my chairing the New England Peace Studies Association, serving on Fellowship of Reconciliation's National Committee, and national and international peace studies associations. In process since about 1965, with a few research centers, undergraduate and graduate programs in the US and abroad, by the turn of the century, grew to more than four hundred centers and academic programs around the world. Although I had taught a popular course on the Literature of the First World War, after writing about the same period, I knew very little about scholarship and research on peacemaking in economics, sociology, mathematics, political science and psychology by scholars in various countries, since Johan Galtung founded the first international peace research center in Oslo in 1959.

Meanwhile, local peace activists were maintaining an extended protest at a GTE plant nearby that made the intricate electrical systems for nuclear missiles. In an effort to speak with the workers, we picketed the front gate and along a fence surrounding the plant, committing civil disobedience by walking on to the property. In one of several such incidents six people, including my oldest daughter, Mary Laurel, and I, were arrested and briefly jailed. To our surprise, we were allowed to present a defense, arguing that weapons assembled at GTE were illegal according to international law. The judge, nonetheless, ruled guilty and sentenced us to several hours of community service.

protesters, including Michael at right, undertaking civil disobedience 1986 at GTE plant near Worcester

Joe Egger, Michael, and Colman McCarthy,
a columnist for the Washington Post, *from left*

On campus, the peace and justice committee of interested faculty, campus ministers, and several talented, imaginative students sponsored films, workshops, and speakers, including *Washington Post* journalist Colman McCarthy and César Chavéz, co-founder of United Farm Workers and the most important apostle of nonviolence since Martin Luther King Jr. A student-organized OXFAM banquet, involving their classmates in a dramatization of the world's food supply, was perhaps the most memorable of events. Responding to the American Catholic bishop's pastoral letter, "The Challenge of Peace: God's Promise and Our Response," 1983, calling for peace research at Catholic colleges and universities, students and people from the community responded positively to that initiative, and as a result of its activities, the Committee became the most active organization on campus.

A major campaign at the time, important to our committee, was the exposure of secret US interventions in Central and South America, including massive military aid to dictatorial regimes throughout the region. Our government's response at that time to nationalist rebels, labeled "Communists," amounted to a kind of hysteria, including fears of their

*Arthur Brien, Susin King, Judith Moran, and Michael, from left, at
School of the Americas civil disobedience action in Columbus, Georgia*

making their way to El Paso. Meanwhile, Roy Bourgeois, an American
Maryknoll priest exiled from Latin America for human-rights organizing in
Bolivia, documented the complicity of the US Government in training death
squads responsible for the assassination of four American women, six Jesuits,
and their housekeepers, and Óscar Romero, archbishop of San Salvador. In
its legislative and direct action campaign, School of the Americas Watch,
initiated by Father Bourgeois, gathered thousands of people at the gates of
the School of the Americas, later renamed Western Hemispheric Institute
for Security Studies at Fort Benning, Georgia, to close the facility.
Demonstrations and street theater there involved families of Latin
Americans killed by military personnel trained in torture at Fort Benning,
with a number of elderly American priests and nuns arrested for civil
disobedience and jailed for six months or more. Legislative campaigning in
Washington each April, with strong support from my local Congressman,
James McGovern, urged Congress to cut funding for School of the Americas,
even as the US increased military aid to Colombia and paramilitaries in
Latin America in order to terrorize and kill many innocent people.

Particularly memorable events in our committee's ten-year history included presentations by Penny Lernoux, an award-winning journalist whose work focused on the persecution of the Catholic Church, the murder of priests and nuns by paramilitaries and dictators, often supplied with armaments from the US; Maryknoll Sister Bernice Kita, who worked among peasants in Guatemala, before accompanying Mayan peoples seeking asylum from the war, to Mexico; and the film *Romero*, perhaps the most powerful religious film I have ever seen, about the ministry of Oscar Romero and his martyrdom in 1989. The late Howard Zinn, before an audience of two hundred students, colleagues and townspeople, spoke with customary wit and simplicity about the history of nonviolent struggle, responding to hostile questions in a manner that further engaged the audience.

Shortly after Howard's visit to campus, his friend Daniel Berrigan returned to read three new fables: "The War Between the Ants and the Elephants," "The Void" about MX missile silos, and "The Making of a Camel" about the American bishops' peace pastoral letter. Tom Lewis, Dan's Catonsville Nine compatriot and Worcester resident, drove Dan from Logan Airport, Boston, and arrived late with Tom's weary Volkswagen bus running aground before Blessed Virgin Mary's statue at the front of the campus. Daniel described his recently being hauled before the Jesuit provincial in New York, accompanied by the superior of his community, after they advocated using churches as sanctuaries for war resisters unsuccessfully. Daniel persisted as a peace activist and wrote fifty books and innumerable lectures, including an anthology I edited, *Daniel Berrigan: Poetry, Drama, and Prose,* 1988. His activism led to repeated arrests for civil disobedience against weapons of mass destruction. As he returned to New York from Assumption, I remember his face appearing somewhat tragic as he boarded an early morning flight at Logan Airport for Manhattan, but his body and disposition at seventy remained youthful.

At home, family life remained equally, if not more eventful in the years between our return from China and further travels abroad over the next two decades. Concerned that our children might feel pressured to achieve academically, because of the heavy emphasis on formal education in New England particularly among academics, I was happy that they managed to survive their high school years unscathed. Rightly or wrongly, we allowed them to follow their own choices in education, even as several transferred within the system or dropped in and out of college. The three younger children had the opportunity of attending Baker River School in New Hampshire, thanks to the generosity of Betsy and Bruce Bergquist. Their guidance and innovative approach to education helped Chris, Anne, and Betsy to identify their talents so that they flourished later on. As children of faculty, ours could attend Assumption tuition free, but all of them chose to go elsewhere, where they concentrated variously as undergraduates and graduate students in Spanish, math, philosophy, fine arts, history, and English at ten colleges and universities in six states. After John and Mary Julie's wedding in 1984, the other children—Mary Laurel, Michael, Betsy, Chris—married, with Annie joining her partner as well. By 2005, ten grandchildren—Jonathan, Juliann, Shannon, Dan, Laurel, Alison, Elizabeth, Liam, Brigid, and Emmett—further enriched out lives, with the extended family eventually numbering twenty-four.

On temporary leave from Assumption prior to 1997, I happily accepted invitations to teach at Colorado College, Holy Cross College in Worcester, Worcester Polytechnic Institute, and for a semester at the University of Hawaii, Manoa. Those assignments enabled me to work with colleagues in established peace studies programs and to gain experience relevant to the program in progress at Assumption. Through those assignments and professional organizations, I became acquainted with a whole range of research on the efficacy of peacemaking, in resolving conflict in the family, schools, and wider community, though I was slow to learn essential skills and strategies essential to nonviolent communication and mediation, direct action, and nonviolent intervention. My involvement in the International Peace Research Association or IPRA and its US affiliate increased my knowledge of peace studies but reinventing myself as a Johnny-come-lately social scientist was hard work. Although my background in literature and history was helpful, developing introductory courses was particularly demanding, since they were truly interdisciplinary.

Teaching at Colorado College, the only American college with a minor in nonviolence, I relied on members of a vibrant Catholic Worker-Mennonite community, particularly a priest, Steve Handen, which proved to be a boon for my course and the students. Laicized and married, Steve and his wife, Mary Lyn, an artist, had initiated a soup kitchen for homeless people in downtown Colorado Springs years before and devoted themselves to nonviolent social change and the corporal and spiritual works of mercy, with remarkable and sustained effectiveness. With others, they offered hospitality to immigrants from Latin America while maintaining a bicycle repair shop, free to young people, organizing demonstrations, the First Strike Theater, and committing disobedience against war makers that surround the city: the United States Air Force Academy, Jefferson Air Force Base, Fort Carson, as well as the North American Aerospace Defense Command, NORAD, the underground hideout for military personnel in the event of nuclear attack, and several secret security installations. Although Colorado Springs, home to forty organizations of the religious right, remains a hotbed of religious conservatism, with a newspaper of similar persuasion, local citizens maintain a grudging respect for the Catholic Worker-Mennonite community and Pikes Peak Peace and Justice Commission. They even elected Steve to the local draft board.

A strong liberal arts college, with a national student body, Colorado College followed the block plan, whereby students took one course at a time for three and a half weeks. The plan had been successful for about twenty years, enabling the college to hire artists, filmmakers, and others with special interests for that period. As Sheffer Visiting Professor of Religion, I taught a course in religion and literature that led to my being invited back several times to offer a course on nonviolence. On each occasion, I leaned heavily on Steven, who eventually took over the course, providing students with opportunities for community service and learning concrete skills about nonviolent solutions. During one block, interested faculty, the college chaplain, and local activists arranged talks by Elise Boulding, Howard Zinn, and local activists including First Strike Theater and a geology professor's workshop on aikido, the Japanese martial art. For the last meeting of a course on nonviolence, the class gathered in a circle on a knoll at the center of the campus, with Pikes Peak in the distance, responding to Jon-Kabat Zinn's mindfulness meditation book, *Wherever You Go, There You Are,* a fitting conclusion to a particularly rich assembly of discussions and class presentations.

Gradually, anthologies of syllabi on various approaches for the interdiscipline became available, while the United States Institution for Peace, Washington, helped to extend public discourse on issues of war and peace. Participating in IPRA conferences in Kyoto, Malta, Seoul, Brisbane, Sopron, and Calgary and co-chairing the national affiliate, COPRED, I seized the opportunity to work closely with Johan Galtung, Kenneth and Elise Boulding, and Chad Alger. I co-chaired IPRA's Nonviolence Commission with Chaiwat Satha-Anand, Thammasat University, Bangkok and co-edited a book with him and two talented younger scholars from various disciplines attracted to the area of study.

My slide presentation, "The American Tradition of Nonviolence," traced the tradition from seventeenth-century Quakers to mid nineteenth-century abolitionists to the late twentieth century disarming of nuclear weapons by Plowshares and took me literally around the world from Groningen University, the Netherlands, to the University of Canterbury, Christ Church, New Zealand. Needless to say, I was the primary beneficiary of those amazing encounters and discussions, whatever they may have meant to diverse audiences.

Although we seldom hear about the history of nonviolence in school, Howard Zinn's writings have remedied that situation somewhat. Activists around the world discover by trial and error, as with Gandhi's experiments with truth, which of the 198 methods of nonviolent action work or don't work and why, in given contexts. Since 1973, groundbreaking research by Gene Sharp, the greatest theorist of nonviolence since Gandhi, and colleagues at the Albert Einstein Institution, Boston, have provided concrete evidence of successful nonviolent campaigns of the past century and beyond. My favorite rediscovery in that regard was Adin Ballou, 1801-1890, from nearby Hopedale, Massachusetts, who wrote the first extended discourse on nonviolence, *Christian Nonresistance*, in 1846.

The semester before retiring from full-time teaching in August, 1997, I taught courses on nonviolence at the Spark M. Matsunaga Institute for Peace and Conflict Resolution, University of Hawaii, which had established cooperative programs with community groups across the state. On the day of a major US offensive in the Middle East, I participated in a memorable Martin Luther King Day Celebration with James Farmer, the

Michael, front right, top, and Michael and Mary Pat, right, above, with colleagues in Hawaii

distinguished civil rights leader. At a television interview, amid all flags waving and speaking fast and furiously, I emphasized how our foreign interventions violated international law. My surprised host hurriedly ended our conversation and sent me on my way.

Living on the beautiful university campus on Oahu for a semester was obviously a gift in itself. Amenities included a walk to class each morning among gorgeous tropical plants, with Waikiki Beach only a short bus ride from my office. From earlier visits, I had become acquainted with the vital community responsible for Hawaii's academic and activist programs through Professor Glenn Paige, founder of the Center for Global Nonviolence and famous for his commitment to "non-killing political science." Father Berrigan visited and spoke to students about his experience in nonviolent social change, followed by a lively social gathering at an Italian restaurant afterward.

Back home the following fall, I gradually became aware of the effect the events prior to my retiring had on me—particularly the intransigence and narrowness, both academic and religious, of the college president. Earlier, he had disparaged several other faculty members and me for questioning his judgment on academic matters. His imposition of a narrow curriculum had also led to the faculty voting a loss of confidence in his administration. Little by little, however, the president got what he wanted, even as students expressed their displeasure with a curriculum that made it almost impossible, among other things, for them to double-major.

As the president moved to the right politically and theologically, becoming "more Catholic than the pope," he allied himself with the Knights of Malta and similar reactionary organizations and took to wearing costumes with plumes, swords, and elaborate medals resembling those of Latin American dictators. A similar retrenchment by the Vatican and Catholic hierarchy began to affect Catholic institutions of higher learning, generally, while the army of so-called Catholic intellectuals remained silent.

Although the president had once regarded me as a dear friend (I have it in writing) and occasionally took me to lunch at the Worcester Club, he began attacking me in print, all the while surrounding himself with toadies beholden to him for perks and higher salaries. Although I felt sorry for him, as he never knew quite what to do with me, I managed to ignore him most of the time; my grown children, however, deeply resented his public criticism. In the face of it all, not one of my colleagues at Assumption came to my defense publicly.

When David O'Brien, a close friend at Holy Cross, wrote an Op-Ed in my defense, the *Worcester Telegram and Gazette*, where my writings appeared over many years, refused to publish it, perhaps because the editor was friendly with the president. The editor of the *Catholic Free Press*, for which I had written for years, responded similarly, telling David that, though he wanted to publish the piece, the chair of his board, wife of the Assumption president, wouldn't allow it. In a final insult the president turned down the English department's recommendation that I retire as professor emeritus, a strictly honorary title, but meaningful to me nonetheless. Determined not to play his ridiculous game or to criticize him publicly, I went to his office shortly before leaving campus to thank him for what he had done for me over the years, including awarding a scholarship to the daughter of my colleague from China.

Probably as a result of a colleague's shenanigans, as the president awarded him an honorary degree, the college uncharacteristically held no retirement party acknowledging my thirty-two years on the faculty. I regretted that, since it prevented my bidding a fond farewell to staff who had been so kind to me over the years. Faithful friends and colleagues, nevertheless, organized a gala event for Mary Pat, who retired at the same time as a school psychologist, and me at a local union hall.

That fall, David Christianson, a remarkable linguist and one of my dearest colleagues, died suddenly. Shortly afterward I learned of the death of Denise Levertov, whose magnificent poems sustained me over the years. In her last note to Mary Pat and me a month before she died, Denise mentioned the "mixed blessing of a whole audience singing 'Happy Birthday' to me after my reading at Goshen College. Such a silly unmusical song but such a nice gesture." Her death, at seventy-four, was a huge loss to

American poetry and to her audience, including many admirers and friends indebted to her courage as an engaged artist and generous person. A selection of her poems, *The Stream and the Sapphire,* which includes religious poems comparable to the lyrics of the metaphysical poets Donne and Herbert, appeared soon afterward.

Preparing lectures for forthcoming courses in India, as well as relishing the fact that I would soon be there, was a good distraction. I soon realized that the negative effects of events around my retirement had wounded me in a way that I couldn't explain. Ironically, only two months later, the president, one of the pope's gentlemen-in-waiting, left in a scandal. A year later, the new president signed a faculty petition affirming my appointment as professor emeritus. Since teaching at colleges and universities in the US and abroad over the next four years greatly enriched my personal and professional life, I never regretted retiring early from my full-time position.

INDIA AND LATIN AMERICA

Jump into experience while you are alive!
Think . . . and think . . . while you are alive.
What you call "salvation" belongs to the time
    before death.

—sixteenth-century Indian poet Kabir
translated by Robert Bly

Each time I returned home from India, I had a hard time conveying to
others the value and richness of my time there. A complicating factor was
that, whenever I described that experience, a still, small voice whispered in
my ear: "You lie!" Did all those adventures really happen to me: falling
from a bus the day Sonya Gandhi drew huge crowds for a political rally in
Bhubaneswar; slicing my thumb on a rusty door latch in the Netaji
Subhash Chandra Bose International Airport, Kolkata, before flying to
Goa for a gathering of Fulbrighters; seeing Arundhati Roy at a film festival
at the Max Muller Bhavan in Delhi, after she was awarded the Booker
Prize for Literature.

Such were the sights and sounds of India, as I negotiated my way
through an ancient, conflicting, and multifarious culture: the beauty of
Belur Math, the principal Vedanta center, and the Ramakrishna Mission at
Gol Park, Kolkata; afternoon tea at the Raj Hotel overlooking the Gate of
India and the harbor in Mumbai; the confusion of buses, cars, bicycles,
cows, trucks, motorbikes, and pedestrians on the narrow road between
Varanasi and Sarnath, between Bhubaneswar and Kolkata; and the awe
and wonder of being at the convergence of the Indian Ocean, Arabian Sea,
and Bay of Bengal in Kanyakumari at the end of the continent.

An Anuvrat Global Organization or ANUVIBHA conference on
nonviolence at Jain Vishva Bharati Institute (Deemed University), Ladnu,

Rajasthan, had brought me to India for the first time in 1995. There, eighty men and women, including UN officials, journalists, and scholars from eighteen countries joined two hundred monks, nuns, faculty, students, and residents, and His Holiness Ganadhipati Tulsi for four days focusing on the theme, "Living in Harmony with Nature: Survival into the Third Millennium." On my arrival in Delhi, my dear friend Mahendra Kumar, editor of *Gandhi Marg,* arranged for me to stay at the guest house, Delhi University, after I hobbled with an attack of gout from the Gandhi Center to Connaught Place, then hired a pedicab to take me to look for medication to relieve the pain.

Returning home from the conference, I applied for a Fulbright teaching fellowship in American literature. That assignment enabled me to teach six weeks at Utkal University in the eastern part of India, as well as take part in peace, conflict, and nonviolence studies at the Gandhi Institute, University of Rajasthan, in the west and for extended visits to Kolkata, Delhi, and Goa.

Preparations for the first teaching assignment occupied most of my time during the fall of 1997, rereading poems and novels and writing lectures, arranging for a visa and vaccinations, and gathering anthologies and literary works to be assigned once I arrived. On Christmas Day, two days before flying to Delhi, probably as a result of my medication for malaria, I was staggered by a high fever and feelings of disorientation. Thinking I might not be able to make the journey, I decided that if it didn't work out, I could simply return home. After that decision, things fell into place.

Arriving in Delhi on my first extended stay in India, I spent three days at the YWCA, then in an apartment next door to the Fulbright Office, a handsome colonial building surrounded by tropical plants and trees near Connaught Place and Bengali Market. The staff at United States Education Foundation of India, USEFI, were inordinately helpful and cooperative, guiding me to appropriate officials and organizations and arranging my travel. The military personnel in uniform at the bank, when I cashed my paycheck, were disconcerting, but moving about the city by pedicab was relatively easy.

From Delhi, I flew through Kolkata to Bhubaneswar, the capital of Orissa, on the Bay of Bengal, on the eastern shore. Declining an invitation to spend the first night at a five-star hotel, I took up residence in modest quarters at Hotel Urmi, about two miles from the campus of Utkal University. It proved to be the right place for me, with plain, decent food, and a quiet atmosphere. A journal entry recorded one evening when I first arrived indicates, however, that memories of events surrounding the previous fall remained a burden:

> I have hit bottom, not rock bottom, but certainly basement level. I am not desperate, but I am empty and puzzled and lonely. That is not a new feeling, since I have been plagued by similar anxieties since my retirement in August; after Dave Christianson's death September 25, it returned with a vengeance. Perplexed, I thought seriously of resigning the Fulbright fellowship, but managed to throw myself into preparations for teaching Whitman, Frost and Eliot. Ignoring hesitations and fears, I plunged ahead. Looking back, I realize that I was hardly "there," practicing a face, in response to unseen and unexpected negative energy. The college's "under-developed ego," personified by people's provincialism and lack of awareness, remains a negative factor, and does harm. Feigning impartiality and "Christianity," remaining passive aggressive, they pretend "things aren't so bad," at the expense of themselves and one another. One must challenge that atmosphere by drawing the line and responding with active clarity.

The morning after writing that entry, I woke feeling that everything would be fine, the first such awakening in months. The window of my second-floor hotel room looked down at a compound next door, with corrugated metal roof, a palm tree, and tropical plants in bloom. In the early morning, men, women, and adolescents wrapped in sarongs, stood in line, then under a cold water spigot. In a shaded corner nearby, others poured water from a tin tub over themselves or waited in the open, a towel over his/her shoulders. The compound, just off the busy, two-lane, second busiest thoroughfare in the country, is home to twenty people busy with washing clothes and preparing meals, the children at play. A morning haze slowly gives way to sunny weather, though dustier throughout the day, until evening.

After breakfast, on my way to the campus, I walked along the busy highway to catch a ramshackle, rusty yellow bus, as school children in uniforms filled the metal two-seaters on either side of the aisle. The driver struggled with the long, bent gear shift as he maneuvered through heavy traffic—huge trucks, cars, buses, and motorbikes weaving from one lane to another at the whim of the driver, trying to avoid occasional cows or goats. I sat on the side opposite the highway, since it looked as if we were in imminent danger of colliding with vehicles coming toward us. Along the way, families living in small, low tents without electricity or other amenities gathered around leaky water mains to bathe or to wash their clothes. As we approached the main gate of the university, known as Vani Vihar, students arrived at Orissa's leading institution of higher learning, on foot or by scooter or pedicab on their way to classrooms and lecture halls.

In a large, bare room, just beyond the iron gate to the English department, classes began rather casually. Students in modern American poetry were intrigued by the poems of Walt Whitman and Robert Frost and of more recent poets unfamiliar to them—William Carlos Williams, Allen Ginsberg, and Denise Levertov. T. S Eliot was reputed to be the best-known writer in English after Shakespeare. So I took some delight in telling them that Eliot, born in St. Louis, regarded himself a writer in the American grain, even as he altered the landscape of English literature. I delighted in my relationship with the students and their responses to what we read. My artist son Christopher responded to my saying as much in letters home,

> One of the things mom mentioned that interested me was how
> much you have enjoyed digging into literature again. Isn't it great to
> rediscover the old loves of your life? Sometimes when I am teaching
> my students about an artist or technique, I am suddenly transported.

Adapting to the university's plain, colorless buildings and flat, dusty landscape as well as the unavailability of resources found at American colleges, I appreciated the department chair letting me pretty much make my own way and inviting me to his campus home several times. In addition to teaching, I gave lectures on literature and the United States and read poetry to audiences on and off campus.

The chairman's son and his friend drove me around town on the back of a motor bike sans helmet, my survival a matter of luck. Although Bhubaneswar is a relatively "new" city, the capital of Orissa, its history was evident in the numerous ancient temples and landmarks. One afternoon, the young men drove me to Puri, on the Bay of Bengal, the location of a major place of religious pilgrimage. On the way, we visited a shrine dedicated to Asoka, the great emperor who reigned over much of the country a thousand years before. After a career of conquest and killing, he converted to Buddhism and renounced violence. A new plaque near a stupa restored by Japanese Buddhists paid tribute to him, referring also to "man's inhuman craze for nuclear weapons which might end the world."

In several visits to Kolkata 150 miles north, I benefited from the kindness of Dr. Uma Das Gupta, my Fulbright supervisor, a distinguished historian and biographer of the poet Rabindranath Tagore. She took me to Belur Math, the principal monastery of the Ramakrishna Order, which, unlike similar places in India, was well cared for. Joining pilgrims, their hands folded in prayer, we walked toward the ghat at the Hooghly River, where a thin, elderly man stood waist-deep in the river and another man in wet shorts turned and wrapped himself in a sarong.

Later, when we entered the temple, Uma prostrated herself before an image of Ramakrishna, the Bengali saint, then knelt before Swami Bhuteshananda, ninety-seven-year old guru and principal, who welcomed us cordially. Speaking haltingly, he gave each of us two pieces of candy. In the bookshop, a poster of Vivekananda, Ramakrishna's principal disciple, who created a sensation at the 1892 World Congress of Religions in Chicago, quoted his remark about service to others being the work of God. As an admirer of Christopher Isherwood's novel *Meeting at the River,* set at Belur Math, and biographer of Ramakrishna, I was aware of the novelist's presence there and at Ramakrishna Mission, a kind of oasis at Gol Park on the south side of Kolkata, where I resided.

Another afternoon, Dr. Das Gupta invited me to tea at the Bengal Club to meet her friend, Niladri Chatterjee, a handsome young college teacher and former Fulbright scholar at the University of Texas, Austin. Because of our shared admiration of Isherwood, Niladri having written about him and having met his partner, we had much to talk about. Niladri also invited me to visit his class in American poetry at Kalyani University forty miles north of the city. The four hour ride, through narrow lanes and small villages, was an adventure in itself as cows moved around and through heavy traffic, causing long delays along the route. An excellent rapport between Niladri and his students on my arrival contributed to our lively discussion about American life and literature. Fortunately, our return to the city by train took only about a fourth of the time getting there.

I enjoyed meeting several of Niladri's young friends and appreciating the country and its culture, including the younger generation. Dr. Das Gupta also arranged for me to spend a night at the Bengal Club, its English colonial pretensions a shadow of its former self. Remnants of the elaborate furnishings appeared a bit tattered, as did the older attendants in uniforms from days gone by. Even in its frumpiness, there was something rather elegant about the club and the Park Street bookstores, shops, and restaurants down the street and around the corner.

My Kolkata residence, the Ramakrishna Mission, is the main office and library of the Vedanta Society with a lush flower garden encircled by a four-story building. Outside my window on the first floor, children of various ages played along the crumbling sidewalk and metal fence amid dusty, dark green flowers. A boy about eight years old pulled a cart as three younger children, happy at play, ran behind, then piled on, pushing one another. Their thin legs and haunches spoke of deficiencies as they laughed and shouted their way along the street as a barefoot boy ran behind them.

After lively conversation with English teachers at Kolkata University, Dr. Das Gupta arranged for me to give the slide presentation on nonviolence at the Indian Institute of Management and to speak on a panel with the distinguished economist Amlan Datta.

A few days later, I flew to Bangladesh to participate in a centenary celebration marking the birth of William Faulkner. At Dhaka University, the observation included a remembrance by the son of one of Faulkner's closest friends. As a guest of the Chamber of Commerce, I moved quickly through security at the airport and rode around town with American embassy staff. For the second time in my life, I stayed at a five-star hotel. One afternoon, after speaking to children of industrialists and foreigners at the International School in Dhaka, I was driven to a university twenty miles north on roads about twenty feet above the rich alluvial ground. This engineering feat was a concession to the likelihood of the many rivers flooding a landscape well below sea level.

For an annual gathering of Fulbrighters, fifty lecturers, and talented young students studying Sanskrit, Carnatic music, and Indic religions, I flew back across India to a resort in Goa, on the Arabian Sea. The exotic locale and scenery contrasted sharply with my usual accommodations, including sleeping on an iron bed in a bare room. My elaborately furnished brick cottage, at a resort owned by the Raj Hotel Corporation, was luxurious by any standard, especially when compared with standard dwellings of most people in India.

Having completed my assignment in Bhubaneswar, in March, I flew to Jaipur, "the pink city," in Rajasthan, the largest state in India, bordering Pakistan. At the insistence of Naresh Dadhich, a political science professor at the University of Rajasthan, I stayed with him, his wife, Rita, and their extended family while teaching at university's Center for Gandhian Studies. Each morning, I walked with Manmohan, Naresh's father, a retired public official and a Gandhian, meeting and speaking with his friends in a garden of green shrubs, petunias, zinnias, and nasturtiums nearby. In the evening, as the weather grew warmer, we sat on the balcony with a view of the surrounding hills and desert. Celebrating Holi, one of numerous religious holidays, the Dadhich children, my daughter, Anne, who was visiting at the time, and I "threw" colors—red, yellow, and blue dyes mixed with water—to mark the beginning of spring. Across the street, a young mother worked out of a shed, folding clothes, as three small

135

Michael aboard an elephant in Jaipur, India

children played at the edge of the street or beneath a plank that served as her ironing board.

Two blocks from that middle-class neighborhood, with wide streets and a cosmopolitan air, families lived in shabby pup tents beside the sidewalk, cooking food in pots at little fires in the dirt. Mothers, in colorful, torn saris, walked the streets with a child on each hip and other small children by her side, their bare feet crusted with mud and their hair tangled. Simple sheets draped around poles are the only "walls" separating families from the elements, the traffic and passersby. Returning to Jaipur at Naresh's invitation over the next twelve years, I found them living in the same conditions.

My students at the Gandhi Center at the university pursued graduate degrees, some focusing on nonviolence; as with many educated people in India, they were fluent in English and several national languages. Occasionally, I found myself staring at students, with their handsome visage-dark eyes, high coloring,-and beautiful attire. S. L. Gandhi, ANUVAT's executive director, whom I met earlier, arranged a meeting with members of a wealthy Jain community. Touring the city, I visited famous shrines and historic sites in the region and a large market where I bought shawls for my wife and daughters back home. With its broad streets and desert vistas, Jaipur was spacious, unlike other major cities, and Rajasthani art, architecture, and vibrant stone coloring gave it a distinctive character. A fort just outside the city, where I rode an elephant in the courtyard, was one of several in a region invaded by tribes from the west centuries earlier.

On a third trip five years later, a Fulbright fellowship enabled me to survey programs in peace, conflict, and nonviolence studies at major universities in Delhi, Varanasi, Mumbai, Chennai, Chandigarh, in addition to schools in Nagercoil and Bangalore. In Delhi, Professor Mahendra Kumar again arranged for me to stay at the university guesthouse, where monkeys from the park nearby gamboled outside my room. By coincidence, on a flight from Delhi to Kolkata two weeks later, I sat beside Surandan Das, Vice Chancellor, University of Kolkata, whose driver took me to the Ramakrishna Mission, which again served as my local residence. My duties there included meetings with university faculty in peace and conflict studies and graduate students in American literature, and giving a slide presentation on nonviolence before a sizable international audience at the posh, but heavily guarded American Center. In entering the compound, we had to walk through crowds demonstrating against American policy in Iraq. The war was a frequent topic of conversation in question periods at the Center, and later at the USAS center and the home of embassy staff in Dhaka. After I acknowledged my opposition to United States policy in the Middle East, audiences seemed to relax before asking insightful questions about American life and culture.

A week on the campus of Banaras Hindu University, Varanasi, a major institution with law and medical schools, gave me an opportunity to tour the famous ghats along the Ganges River, as well as Deer Park, Sarnath, where the Buddha, following his enlightenment, gathered his first disciples. My hostess, Professor Chandrakala Padia, a brilliant scholar of political science, made my week on campus particularly memorable, arranged meetings with students and faculty in women's studies and the university president, who was knowledgeable in his analysis and frank in his critique of American imperialism.

In a trip to the far south, I spent a week both in Chennai, capital of Tamil Nadu on the southeastern coast, and spoke at the university, which had a strong interdisciplinary program in conflict resolution. Benjamin, a Catholic whom I met through an Assumption colleague, drove me out to visit the Krishnamurti compound, then to his home for dinner with his wife, Mary, and their family. As head of the Slum Development Society, Benjamin, a dhalit, regularly traveled to the hill country, north of Chennai to acquaint village people with citizen's rights and benefits. After an afternoon at the Gandhi Peace Foundation, among teenagers learning to do mediation through role play, I traveled further south by way of Trivandrum, capital of Karala, but my campus engagement was canceled because of a student strike.

Because of my dear friends, S. P. Udayakumar, his wife, Meera, and their young sons Satya and Surya, my week on the southernmost coast was truly magical. Kumar and I had met years before at the University of Hawaii, when he was completing a doctorate in political science; later on a fellowship at the University of Minnesota Law School, Kumar, Meera, and my daughter, Mary Laurel, became friends, before they returned to initiate an elementary school in Nagercoil. While I was there, they took me to an historic Hindu temple on the way to Kanyakumari, at the far end of the continent. Taking off our shoes and shirts, as is the custom, we walked through dark passageways past altars and statues in an atmosphere that was both mysterious and genuinely holy. In the late afternoon, a short boat ride took us to a small island from which Vivekananda launched his ministry as a disciple of the great Vedanta saint, Ramakrishna.

Although Americans had assured me that Gandhi was hard to find in India, I soon discovered that they had not been paying attention. Throughout the country, one came upon boulevards named for him, statues of him and institutions dedicated to him, including the Gandhi museum at the Raj Ghat in Delhi, not to mention centers on thirty university campuses and in major cities. Lectures and conferences on Gandhi in India tended to be ceremonial rather than educational, and all Indians seemed to regard themselves as authorities on the Mahatma simply because of their nationality. Although adults were anxious to discuss their particular take on his life and legacy, they were surprisingly ignorant of his influence on nonviolent movements and activists around the globe: Martin Luther King, Daniel and Philip Berrigan, and César Chavéz in the US as well as heroic figures responsible for democratic social change in the Philippines, China, South Africa, Latin American, and Eastern Europe.

Through Dr. N. Radhakrishnan, former director of Gandhi Bhavan in Delhi, where the Mahatma spent his last hundred days, I spent an afternoon with his compatriots who also maintain training centers in nonviolence for young people in Kerala. At the International Center for Gandhian Studies and Research near the Raj Ghat, where Gandhi, Nehru, his daughter Indira Gandhi, and grandson Rajiv Gandhi are buried, sixty teachers gathered for two five-hour conversations following my presentation, "People Power: The Story of Global Nonviolence Since 1980." Gandhi's association with Banaras Hindu University and Jamia Millia Islamic University, as well as almost everywhere I traveled throughout the country, deepened my appreciation of his constructive programs. His contributions to Indian culture and its people, long under British domination, enabled them to take pride in their history and to reclaim their self-esteem. In supporting workers, liberating untouchables, and encouraging an ecumenical spirit among religions, he achieved much more than independence for India and its people.

Gandhi's legacy was brought home to me in a memorable meeting with Pratibha Patil, governor of Rajasthan, when beneath a gigantic painting of Gandhi, she welcomed us to the Raj Bhavan in Jaipur. As a child, Mrs. Patil and her parents had actively supported Gandhi's Freedom Movement. She obviously approved of Nasresh's commitment to Gandhian studies, and later appointed him vice-chancellor of a large state university. Two years after our first meeting, she invited Naresh and me to her office in Delhi soon after she was elected the first woman president of India.

Michael with Pratibha Patil, president of India, 2007

Walking up the long steps leading to Rashtrapati Bhavan, the president's palace, and down the long hall to her office, I remembered a scene in Richard Attenborough's great film, *Gandhi*. Following his successful nonviolent campaign in 1930 challenging the British tax on tea, Gandhi had walked up those same steps to meet the British Viceroy of India just seventeen years before independence. During his fifty-year-long campaign, which he referred to as his "experiments with truth," Gandhi revived and strengthened a nonviolent tradition that has benefited millions of people.

My travels throughout India usually coincided with milder weather, December to March, before the temperatures of late spring reached from 80 to 110 degrees, and at one point, in Mumbai, 118 degrees. As a native of the southwest, I was used to hot weather, but nothing in my experience prepared me for two summer visits to Rajasthan. There, water is scarce, except for the area round Kota and Chambal River, a four-hour drive south of Jaipur. My two trips to Kota included a teacher's institute and

Gandhi conference at Vardhman Mahaveer Open University, where Naresh Dadhich is Vice Chancellor. On the return drive to Jaipur, we spent several hours at a massive hillside fort in Bundi, widely known for its artwork. Although the palace and fortress remain in disarray, the brilliant turquoise and gold murals of ancient myths, gods, and goddesses conveyed something of the majesty of a former princely state.

Centenary celebrations of the publication of Gandhi's *Hind Sawarj* (Indian self-rule), a seventy page booklet, brought me to India in January, 2009 and again a year later. Preparations for and events while I was there increased my appreciation of Gandhi until his death in 1948, his indebtedness to his native culture, and his borrowings from the West. At a seminar in Ajmer, a sacred city of pilgrimage among Sufis, and a conference in Jaipur, entitled "Hind Swaraj of Mahatma Gandhi: Satyagraha Peace Education and Governance," the seven hundred people in attendance represented a range of opinions, which led to heated discussion about the practicality and achievements of nonviolent direct action. Some adults at the conference, as with my students and other young Indians, remained apologists for violence, even though they regard Gandhi as the father of their country.

In numerous publications, his collected works filling one hundred volumes, Gandhi repeatedly challenged the people of India to resist British rule, while distinguishing between the destabilizing violence of modernism and capitalism and the achievements of Western thought. Written on board ship returning from England to South Africa in 1909, at forty, *Hind Sawarj* repeats criticisms that he made earlier in Parliament, when he criticized the British for their failure to govern themselves and their colonies according to the principles of parliamentary democracy.

The concept, swaraj, locates power, including self-discipline, in the individual, in calling everyone to an "age of democracy" and "age of awakening of the poorest of the poor." Relying on "soul force, the power of good in each person and a link with all creation," he called upon the people to assert their dignity in the face of violence and dehumanization under British rule. Through satyagraha, rather inadequately translated into

English as passive resistance, they could affirm and transform his country's rich heritage in the struggle for independence.

Although familiar with those basic concepts, until recently I failed to appreciate the implication of them to Gandhi's religious sensibility. His borrowings from various traditions and respect for traditions other than his own are evident in his writings about God and his favorite hymn, John Henry Newman's "Lead, Kindly Light." A 1927 essay, "God Is,"represents Gandhi's modest though inordinately sophisticated response provoked by a journalist's sardonic remark about Gandhi's "God stunt" in his writing on nonviolence. Although he repeatedly acknowledged his inability to prove God's existence, he put his trust in "an unseen Power which makes Itself felt and yet defies all proof, because it is unlike all that I perceived through the senses." Nor could he account for "evil's existence," which God allows while remaining untouched by it. And although he cautioned us "not to expect certainties in this world, amid perpetual change and contingency," Gandhi held fast to his belief that "God is Truth and Truth is God."

Throughout my time there, except for cutting my thumb on a rusty door handle and banging my head in a fall from a bus, I got along fine in India, no matter what the weather, food, or exigencies of travel. It was the culture shock of returning to the West that sometimes threw me for a loop. On one flight home, for example, I arrived in "the First World," that is Schipol Airport, Amsterdam, in time for breakfast. After boarding the plane for Boston, I was obscenely ill, vomiting, then fainting in the narrow confines of the men's room, somewhere over the Atlantic. Friends back home later accused me of staging the whole scene in order to get bumped to first class and on landing being wheeled through customs at Logan Airport in a wheelchair. Another time, flying through Mumbai on the way to Hamburg, I caught sight of the huge slum just off the runway so familiar to audiences from the opening scenes of the movie *Slumdog Millionaire*.

A later leave taking, however, was more representative of my experience in India, the people I met, and the affection they evoked. It involved Gopal, a young man who accompanied me to and remained with me at the airport when a flight was delayed and whose openness and attentiveness reminded me of previous encounters there. Born and raised in a small village in Rajasthan, he was the first person in his village to attend college, later completing a doctorate in city planning. His father, like everyone else in the village, made a life farming the arid land and tending several sheep and goats, a camel, and a cow. In a vast desert stretching to the Pakistani border, people seldom ventured far from home. Gopal himself traveled the forty miles to and from Jaipur by bicycle. A college teacher, married and with a family, he had made a professional commitment to city planning and community building in his village.

In the years between my first and last visit, changes transformed the urban landscape of India, with its shiny plate glass towers, fancy shops, malls, new terminals and four lane highways between the cities. The noise of modernity—television, cell phones, iPods—is as disruptive of community there as it is in the US. Although the middle class of three million people is as large as our own, an equal number of people in rural and village India remain relatively untouched by its new prosperity. In crowded cities, families huddle at the edge of the road, without water or electricity; children with severed arms beg at intersections. Amid crumbling buildings, where the family wash hangs on fences and piles of refuse accumulates, one comes upon abundant parks, flower gardens, and public works of art. Even poor workers sweeping the streets or digging and piling bricks at a construction site wear multicolored uniforms or saris. In speaking about India, as well as China, almost anything one says about it is true. For that reason, I don't pretend to "portray it," only to mention a few facts and the awe and wonder it evokes for me. My principal memories of India, unlike those of many tourists, are of its beauty. One reason for my emphasizing that fact is that the native dress flatters the human figure of people who are among the handsomest in the world.

Through the turmoil and confusion, an elegance remains, flashing out in surprising ways and leading one to think, as Gandhi did, that India has much to teach. Indians writing in English, including Salman Rushdie and

Amitav Ghosh, dominate the English novel and psychological insights inherent in religious practitioners native to the sub-continent—Buddhists, Jains, Hindus, Sikhs—are essential to interreligious engagement. Or so it seems to me.

In my journal, I once wrote that going to India was one of the gifts of my life.

A decade after retiring from Assumption, I remained friendly with former colleagues, but had little contact with the institution. As with other Catholic colleges, there was some confusion as to whether Assumption was an ecclesiastical or academic institution. A crisis of government and a president who ignored the advice and counsel of the faculty exacerbated the situation, as the faculty constituted the college's strongest element in making decisions and appointments. Unfortunately, the board of trustees ignored the faculty handbook and their responsibility of protecting faculty and students from interference by the state, the church, and corporations, and sided with the president and the religious order that founded the college. In a very professional manner, the faculty challenged the president, but was ignored so that any resolution of the conflict failed. Unfortunately, I could only encourage my former colleagues from a distance in upholding established policy that previously served the college well.

After returning to the US from India, I taught at Colorado College, Holy Cross College, and Worcester Polytechnic Institute, as well as Teachers College, Columbia, and Boston Center for Psychiatric Study. My challenge at the Boston Center was to introduce graduate students, in an intensive part-time program, to peace, conflict, and nonviolence studies. Since they were convinced by argument that human beings were innately violent, they seemed, in fact, silently hostile to anything in conflict with a Freudian perspective on such matters, although a host of anthropologists, psychiatrists, and other scientists in the 1989 *Seville Statement on Violence* had argued that the human brain is not programmed for violence.

The appointment at Columbia University enriched my understanding of peace studies, because of new thought and research, including a new disciplinary approach to pedagogy. Professor Betty Reardon had initiated one of the major programs in peace education twenty years before in the Department of International and Transnational Education. Each week, as during the National Endowment for the Humanities Fellowship at Columbia in 1976 to 1977, I traveled by bus from Worcester to Manhattan on Monday, returning home on Thursday, and stayed in the dorm on campus with little time to move beyond it.

During that time at home, I continued to lecture frequently, to write for publications and to work with the Worcester YWCA Week Without Violence Committee and International Peace Research Association. Professor Ted Herman of Colgate University talked me into chairing the latter organization for two years, which provides grants to scholars engaged in peace research. Bi-lateral yearly IPRA meetings held in Japan, Malta, Australia, South Korea, and Hungary gave me some familiarity with a peace research movement that had become truly international, with several hundred academic programs and research centers around the world. Those initiatives and developments led to the UN Declaration for Peace and Nonviolence for the Children of the World, passed by 189 members of the General Assembly in 1998.

My final adventures abroad took me to South America: people of Colombia, plagued at that time by FARC rebels from the countryside, and people of Argentina, at great risk to themselves, constructed and sustained peace cultures in environments threatened by violence. And shortly after that, I lectured at the Juche Institute in Pyongyang, North Korea.

In Argentina, my host, Alicia Cabezudo, had survived imprisonment and torture during the military junta there, having gathered a community of peace educators in her work with Ciudades Educadoras throughout Latin America. Exiled from her home country for several years, she had narrowly escaped being disappeared under the dictatorship like thirty thousand victims of the purge. By the time we met as colleagues in Betty Reardon's program at Teachers College, Columbia, Alicia had completed a PhD. In addition to being a full professor at the National University of Rosario, she had taught in universities in Europe, Central America, and

South America. When I went to Buenos Aires in 2000, just after Argentina's economic crisis, she had become a valued civil servant as well, working with the regional government in the state of Santa Fe.

Because of Alicia's many associations, I spoke to various groups, including students at the Madres de Plaza de Mayo University, located across from where the mothers had waged a nonviolent campaign demanding an accounting of their sons and husbands disappeared by the military junta. For my lectures and slide presentations on nonviolence at a national congress, a large group of students gathered at the amphitheater in Rosario on the banks of the Rio de la Plata and afterward spoke at a seminar with Santa Fe police officers.

Those invitations obviously reflected Alicia's reputation, which included two meetings with the Socialist mayor of Rosario, later governor of the state.

Through Alicia, I also met her compatriot from Colombia, Amada Benevides, who arranged for me to be in Bogota for several lectures and to Medellin, "the City of Perpetual Spring." Although a State Department travel advisory discouraged Americans from traveling to Colombia because of the rebel incursions, I welcomed the opportunity to visit Medellin, for one of the most moving experiences of my life.

A stunningly beautiful country of mountains and dramatic landscapes, Colombia had had a number of violent raids by rebels, resulting in the assassination of Catholic priests, nuns, and missionaries, and the kidnapping and mutilation of Protestant church workers. Cooperation between the army and brutal paramilitary groups was commonplace, according to Amnesty International. At the same time of periodic rebel disruptions, the US awarded more military aid than for any other country in the world except for Israel and Egypt.

As head of Fundacion Escuelas de Pax, Amada had initiated a nonviolent campaign, in a country victimized by the drug trade by guerrilla bands, who earlier kidnapped her brother for ransom. I spoke to faculty and students at the University in Bogota. In Medellin, known as the center of the drug trade and terrorized by drug lords, Amada and I were guests of

Governor Gaviria, who had provided nonviolence training for his staff throughout the state of Antioquia. His effort was a memorial for Guillermo Gaviria, his brother, who had been kidnapped and murdered after long appeals for his release.

In April 2002, Guillermo Gaviria, then state governor of Antioquia, and Gilberto Echeverri, former defense minister who served as the governor's peace adviser; Bernard Lafayette, the American civil rights leader, and other well-known activists from abroad joined hundreds of farmers and peasants on a march to reclaim an area dominated by drug lords and paramilitaries. During the march, Gaviria, Echeverri, Lafayette, and a Catholic priest sought to meet with the rebels, who instead kidnapped them. Although the rebels quickly released Lafayette and the priest, they murdered Gaviria and Echeverri months later when the national government sent national military officers to rescue them.

While I was there, I spent a day with a former FARC rebel who had renounced violence and managed a community center on the hilly side of the city in one of the poorest areas, where young men learned skills and strategies essential to peacemaking. At a similar center in another part of the city, a young man, who worked to end discrimination against homosexuals, handed me a colorful postcard with a message across the top saying "Kiss me, don't Kill me." Not long after my time in Medellin, Amada was appointed to the UN High Commission on Human Rights, while receiving three death threats for calling attention to and trying to alleviate violence threatening the welfare of her fellow citizens.

After those opportunities to travel, the pattern of my life changed dramatically, as my wife and I sold our home of fifty years and moved into a small retirement community, Goddard House in Worcester. Aging played a part in that, including illnesses and death among family and friends.

My involvement with Quakers for twenty years and the Worcester Interreligious Forum altered my perspective on and understanding of my religious commitment, though not my faith, and led to extensive reading on the world's religions. The main influence may have been my presence in India and my associations and conversations with students, teachers, and citizens, acquainting me with the rich heritage and influence of Hindus, Muslims, Jains, and Buddhists, and a growing familiarity with recent scholarship including Diana Eck's *Encountering God: From Bozeman to Banaras* and books by Karen Armstrong increased my awareness and interest in recent theology as well. Inevitably, that modest spiritual quest led me to reflect on implications regarding my own religious life. Along the way, I read popular books on atheism by Sam Harris and Christopher Hitchens, which sometimes complemented and, in some ways, challenged my reflections on the history of religion. In a marvelous book and series of lectures at Yale, Terry Eagleton's *Reason, Faith, and Revolution* agreed with the atheists' critiques of organized religion, while insisting that the so-called atheists didn't know beans about God.

Recent writings associated with the Jesus Seminar, particularly those of John Dominic Crossan and Marcus Borg, deepened my faith. Focusing on the context and culture in which Jesus lived and combining their knowledge of sociology, medicine, anthropology, history, and linguistics, they fleshed out the sometimes limited and conflicting perspectives of Jesus in the gospels and traditional theologians. Generally I came to agree with the argument of Robert Bellah's *Beyond Belief* and Wilfred Cantwell Smith's *The Meaning and End of Religion* that belief has little to do with religion. Indicating the similarities in the teachings of major religious prophets, those scholars encouraged our focusing not on preparations for the next world, whatever that may be, but on learning how to live fully in this world.

Those insights were common knowledge to many people, particularly people knowledgeable about the teachings of the Buddha, Lao Tzu, and other holy men and women. Slowly I learned to understand them by leaning heavily on the recent rich scholarship and research in religion. It helped to learn that doubt is part of any serious religious quest particularly in a time when we are to account for all the bad news that surrounds us, in the midst of periodic national disasters destroying large areas of the US and the cruelty, ignorance, and incompetence of those in power, the pedophile scandals, deaths, and serious illnesses of friends and family. No wonder people began to wonder if there really is a God or an Ultimate Concern informing the universe (He/She may be almighty, but apparently not in all things).

Each age defines God in a way that meets its needs. Any definite resolution regarding such matters is inevitably tentative, particularly regarding most questions or ultimate concerns—life, death, suffering, love. Eventually, after much reading and experience, I came to the conclusion that, as the theologian Wilfred Cantwell Smith has written, transcendence appears at random times, with intimations of God's existence. So I counted myself a believer, rather than an atheist or agnostic. Convinced, nonetheless, that doubt is an essential element of faith, I agreed with William James that we must allow for "the maybes" that inform our lives. Those issues, values, and choices have a strong hold on my attention and the religious experience of others remains as interesting to me as my own. Although my religious beliefs draw heavily on my early experience, I learned that Catholics seem unnerved by or disinterested in religious concerns beyond their own commitment. A longtime friend fascinated by ecclesiastical politics told me that my interest in interreligious engagement bored him.

WHO I WILL BE BEING

Although I enjoyed good health into my late seventies, several friends were confined to nursing homes with extended care, never to return home. When my two older brothers, Bob, 82, and Herb, 86, died within seven months of one another in March and October of 2009, I felt as if my psyche had been torn away. In spite of my beloved wife and extended family, Herb's death so soon after Bob's was particularly harsh, though I had some consolation in being with Herb in South Bend for two days before he died.

I was then the last member of my immediate family and far from friends who knew me prior to my twenty-fifth birthday: that is, individuals whom I didn't have to explain myself to, who knew my faults and seldom blanched at anything I said. Unfortunately, my involvement in the antiwar and antinuclear movement, my articles and presentations on the arms industry, as well as periodic civil disobedience, led some people to regard me as a type, projecting labels onto me, such as radical, which confused me and distanced me from them.

Writing my memoir offered me an opportunity to avoid losing people and events that have informed and enriched my life. And my travels, as well as my friends and family, were important in understanding my responses to and encounters with a wide range of people.

As my life unfolded, I discovered, in the words of the Neruda poem, not only "how many I am" but "who I will be being."

*John True, Michael True, Mary Laurel True, Betsy True, and Anne True,
from left front, and Christopher True, back, in August 2014*

Michael's Children Remember Him

Jim
McGovern
Democrat ★ Congress

P.O. Box 60405
Worcester, MA 01606-0405
www.jimmcgovern.com

August 5, 2018

Michael TRUE
1199 Main St
Worcester, MA 01603-2012

Dear Michael,

Thank you for your contribution to my re-election campaign. I am grateful for your support and friendship.

The November midterm election is fast approaching and the stakes have never been higher. We must win back the House!

A Democratic victory in the Fall will send a message – loud and clear – that what is happening with this White House and Congress is not normal. It is unacceptable. We need a government that is rational and functional – one that puts the American people first. And we desperately need to return civility and decency to our politics.

Thank you again for your help. Lisa, Patrick, Molly and I wish you and your family all the best.

Sincerely,

Jim McGovern

PS: To keep in touch with my campaign online, please visit JimMcGovern.com, where you'll find links to follow me on Facebook, Twitter and Instagram.

You're the best. I think of you often during these difficult times for our country. Thanks for never giving up and always keeping the faith.

letter and handwritten note to Michael from
US Representative Jim McGovern, D-Worcester

A Life Well Lived

by Mary Laurel True

I have been thinking a lot about what the great peace activist Kathy Kelly said about my father: "Michael True, a life well-lived." So True of that great man!

My dad *loved* life, and he lived life as if his life—and everyone's life—truly mattered.

You knew that you mattered whenever you were with him. He'd say, "Now, Sugar," in his Oklahoma way, "how wonderful it is that you're doing what you're doing. You're just incredible. I wish I could be as good as you are at that."

He'd often quote Thomas Paine's motto, "My country is the world. To do good is my religion." He made that motto his life's mission. Day after day, year after year, and through his writing, teaching, civil disobedience, and encouraging students, resisters, journalists, and friends—one of whom was his own US Congressman, Jim McGovern, he did something about the injustice he saw in the world.

McGovern wrote the following letter to my dad in February, 2019, after hearing my parents had moved to Minnesota:

> Dear Mike,
>
> You are one of my heroes! You are a giant in the peace movement! I am in awe of all your efforts on behalf of non-violence and justice. What an incredible mentor you have been to me and to many in our community (and so many outside our community, as well).
>
> There is still so much to be done. I know we can count on you to continue to be a voice for sanity and common sense.
>
> With respect and friendship,
> Jim McGovern

Being awake as my dad was and constantly resisting oppression as he did were not easy. Some key things kept my father going, and one of them was music. He especially loved an album I had by Iris DeMent. We'd play that CD almost every time we got together, and he'd say, "This is such good writing," and then he'd always do a little dance.

He was a darned good dancer, too!

Love ya, Papa. Hope you're dancing in heaven right now!

No Interest in Some Things

by Michael N. True

First, my father was a reader.

I think that quality or interest skips a generation.

He read everything and had a very wide range of interests. He was a historian, he was a geographer, and he had his interests.

But there were areas where he had no interest. For example, in mechanics or auto mechanics, he had no interest whatsoever. He had no interest whatsoever in carpentry. Even less than either of those, he had no interest in sports.

He especially had no interest in following sports. I know for a fact that he read more poetry while sitting in the bleachers watching one of his kids' one-hour basketball games than I have ever read in my life. Back to sports (though in high school, he was the captain of his small Oklahoma high school basketball team), around 1978, my dad got a call from Indiana State University. They told him that they wanted to interview him for the English department head position. They said they would fly him to Indiana, wine and dine him, and put him up in a nice hotel. From my memory of Terre Haute, that was tough to accomplish. And, they had tickets for him to Larry Bird's last collegiate home game.

My dad responded. "That all sounds great. But who is Larry Bird?"

Back to the auto mechanics—when I was around eight or nine years old, I found my faith in or acknowledgment of a God due to my dad's lack of mechanical ability. We would take cars that most of you in your right mind would not drive the five miles from Minneapolis to St. Paul. My father and mother would drive those cars the fifteen hundred miles from

Worcester to Minnesota. My dad knew where the ignition key went, and that was about the extent of his car knowledge. The cars were not new cars either: they were old, beat-up cars.

At age ten, I had the job of tying the luggage for all eight of us onto the roof of the car. He never checked it. That was my job. And, when it rained, I cleverly figured out that, since we packed our clothes in old suitcases, I wrapped the luggage in a huge tarp. By the time we hit the Mass Pike, that tarp was a sail that barely made it under the overpasses.

There is no way in the world we, the cars, and the luggage would have ever made the three-thousand-mile round trip without divine intervention.

I bought my dad a toolbox a while back and identified the hammer, screwdriver, and pair of pliers, but it never saw much action. Ironically, he did put the tools to some use just a couple of years ago to spruce up the house on 4 Westland Street before they sold it.

He had such a strong commitment to promoting peace. He often cut trips to warm exotic countries short to make it back to Worcester, where it might be cold, raining, or snowing, for his Tuesday standout peace vigil to hold one of the signs, maybe "End All War" or "US Out of Iraq." I remember one time him returning home after a standout vigil. I asked how it went.

In his great academic wisdom and words, he said to me "Well, the finger count is down."

I had no idea what he meant, so I asked, "What do you mean?"

"You know," he responded. "I think that people are getting it. We usually average six or seven people giving us the finger. And today, we only had two give us the finger."

My South Bend, Indiana, cousins shared a story they found wild and I found comical, partly because it was not too rare an occurrence at our house but rare in other households. When I was a twelve and John was ten, we drove through South Bend one weekend on the way to Wisconsin and Minnesota. My dad's brother Herb, his wife, and eight kids lived there. They were often well-dressed and well-coiffed. Our ragtag group of eight showed up to stay for a day, maybe two. Sunday came, and my dad said,

"We are going to Sunday mass." So we all packed up, frantically grabbing what we needed. Herb's kids were ready, well-dressed, hair done up. My family ran around trying to find the bare minimum of shirts, pants, and shoes to wear.

Either my brother John or I could not find our shoes. My dad said, "Forget about it," grabbed us, and carried us into the car. One of us walked into church in a baseball uniform, the other walked in with only one shoe on, and we sat down. As was often the case, my dad was unfazed.

He had a great sense of humor too, and I am sure going to miss him.

"Use Your Imagination."

by John True

"Use your imagination."

That was the last piece of advice my father had for me. As he lay in yet another uncomfortable position in bed at Our Lady of Peace Hospice in St. Paul, the advice came in response to my question to him of how I could assist.

My sister Mary Laurel commented that "use your imagination" was a recurring comment from him over the years. Blessed with a vivid imagination, a wonderful mind, and an indomitable will, he utilized those attributes to make the world a more decent and just place. He received those gifts from his parents, Guy Herbert, called GH, and Agnes Murphy True.

The will came primarily from his mother. By describing her gardening technique in the arid Oklahoma soil, he honored his mother's will and imagination in *Plains Song and Other Poems,* one of his twelve published books. First, she introduced herself to the soil by saying "I'm Agnes Murphy. Now, listen." She then commanded the seeds to grow in clay and dirt soil made famous by John Steinbeck in his Depression-era novel, *The Grapes of Wrath*.

Following her orders, bougainvillea, magnolia, and violets grew and flourished as instructed. If you met Agnes, you would understand that the flowers did just what they had been told to do. Growth is what Agnes wanted, and growth was what it would be.

Tongue in cheek, my dad used to say that he learned conflict resolution and nonviolent strategy from his dad. A gentle and kind man, GH patiently acquiesced with a smile to various directives from Agnes. Sometimes—of course unintentionally—he would not hear her, since his hearing wasn't always great.

My Grandfather True was a happy and content man. He was also a lucky man, having survived being gassed in the Argonne Forest in World War I, not to mention winning a fancy new convertible in a dollar raffle. Fifty years on, I recall his advice to me as if it were yesterday. "Sonny," he'd say, "every morning you wake up, get on your knees, and thank God you are alive." I didn't fully understand the concept at seven years old, but I sure do now.

For my dad as well as his parents, "Use your imagination" was not an abstract request but a necessary skill and call to action. For to survive and thrive in Oklahoma, imagination and action went hand in hand.

To my dad, imagination was important. Imagination, however, without implementation was feeble. He identified feebleness (a favorite word of his) when folks bemoaned the latest atrocity and then did nothing to fix it. "God gave you an imagination to problem-solve," was what he said. "Now, please use it to right the wrong. And for pity sake, don't be feeble in the undertaking. If you want change, get out in the street and use your imagination to plan an effective demonstration so it will make a difference. If the people lead, then politicians will follow." That was his philosophy.

"Use your imagination." Thanks for the sage advice, Dad. Your mother impressively planted her seeds. She taught you well. You have planted seeds for future activists by spending your time mentoring young people and being a role model through your actions. I, personally, will need imagination to move forward without your physical presence in my life. I know, however, you will be with all of us in spirit as you truly are and always will be an "energy force more intense than war."

A Love of Culture

by Christopher True

I'm Mike and Mary Pat's fourth child.

As an artist, I hold an image that's always animated my imagination: the meeting of my parents. When I ask my mother how she and my dad met, which I've done repeatedly over the years just to hear it again, she says, "It was at the Newman Center (the ministry center for Roman Catholic students) at the University of Minnesota. He was playing the piano and singing, and he had a wonderful voice."

One of the great gifts my mother and father have given us is a love of culture, and I think of all the arts, a love of music (especially live music) took deepest root in all six of us kids.

My earliest memories of how they may have instilled a love of the arts and music in us concern great dinner parties my parents hosted. The house that we grew up in at 4 Westland Street had a beautiful maple staircase that went up and around just to the right of a baby grand piano. Those two features were like the heart and lungs of the house.

During dinner parties, we children sometimes sat at the top of the stairs and listened to raucous arguments and conversations ensuing over dinner. The smell of food and wine and pipe tobacco smoke wafted up that staircase, and unlike Bill Clinton, we inhaled—deeply. And occasionally, when the downstairs bathroom was occupied, people came up the staircase and entertained us on their way to the upstairs bathroom.

When dinner ended, everyone came out of the dining room into the entryway and gathered around the piano. We could see them through the curved spaces between the balusters. My dad played show tunes, and everyone sang along. A good singer, my dad had the loudest voice that would sometimes embarrass us in church.

The singing became part of the wonderful rich smell, and we took it all in, and it became part of us.

So, if you're ever looking for us and can't find us, check the Cedar Cultural Center or the Iron Horse, and we'll be there . . . and so will my mom and dad.

Grateful for His Life

by Anne True

In many ways, I dreaded the day of my father's funeral for my whole life. My father meant the world to me and to us, and it is difficult to imagine living in the world without him. But I have to remember what he said often: "We have to keep on keeping on!"

My father was grateful for his life, and he said so often. He had a wonderful life. He was grateful for many things: his family, colleagues, and his adopted city of Worcester. He was also grateful for being able to travel. He gave lectures about nonviolence and peace studies and taught at colleges and universities all over the United States and the world. He spent a year at the University of Nanjing, China, teaching American literature to graduate students. He also went to Gandhi institutes in Jaipur, New Delhi, Mumbai, Bubeneshwar, and other cities in India to give lectures on nonviolence. Although he didn't leave the US until he was forty-five years old, he ended up traveling far and wide, including to North Korea, New Zealand, Australia, Portugal, Spain, Italy, France, England, Colombia, Argentina, and Belgium.

He could travel because he made connections for himself. He created opportunities, he was always working on something, he persisted, and he was an excellent correspondent. Every day he put letters in the mail to people all over the world.

He had a strong foundation, and growing up in Oklahoma, he knew his parents and brothers loved him. Curious, my father took interest in a wide variety of subjects, including poetry, art, literature, religion, history, geography, and politics. He loved to discuss and debate ideas. For me, talking with him felt like being in the reference section of a library, because he was well versed. One of my cousins described him as our "moral compass," I think because my father knew and cared so much about our world and people.

Demanding and determined, he engaged in life and had intense energy and high expectations. He wanted things done right, with thought and class.

Essentially an optimist, my father held strong to his commitment and belief in nonviolence and making the world a more peaceful place. He believed that "we shall overcome, some day!"

He hoped that people would learn from history. He knew that one person can make a difference.

He created a life that he loved and surrounded himself with things that gave him hope: his family, his community, his friends, and people with whom he could discuss issues and books.

Poetry often provided my father with hope and inspiration. He wanted to share his love of poetry and writing by bringing poets to Assumption College or the Worcester Public Library. I'm continually amazed by the number of poets and writers he helped bring to Worcester while at the same time teaching full time in the Assumption English department working on writing his own books and, with my mother, raising six children!

I will end with a list, surely not complete, of people who spoke in Worcester at my father's invitation in the late 1960s through the mid 1990s:

Poets and Writers

Brother Antoninus	James Dickey
Coleman Barks	Stephen Dunn
Ellen Bass	Richard Eberhardt
Wendell Berry	Lawrence Ferlinghetti
Carol Bly	James T. Farrell
Robert Bly	Carolyn Forché
Lucille Clifton	Robert Francis
Sam Cornish	Tess Gallagher
Robert Creely	Chris Gilbert

Poets and Writers
continued

Allen Ginsberg

Louise Glück

Paul Goodman

Donald Hall

Anthony Hecht

Michael Harper

David Ignatow

X. J. Kennedy

Jane Kenyon

Galway Kinnel

Ethridge Knight

Maxine Kumin

Stanley Kunitz

Joseph Langland

John Logan

Meridel Le Seur

Denise Levertov

John Lux

Thomas McGrath

W. S. Merwin

Sharon Olds

Mary Oliver

Grace Paley

Marge Piercy

J. F. Powers

Adrienne Rich

Muriel Rukeyser

May Sarton

Karl Shapiro

Charles Simic

L. E. Sissman

Ken Smith

William Stafford

Mark Strand

Nobel Laureates

Joseph Brodsky

Czeslaw Milosz

Seamus Heaney

Religious/Political Writers

Dan Berrigan

Philip Berrigan

Noam Chomsky

Dorothy Day

Abby Hoffman

Penny Lernoux

John Lewis

Howard Zinn

Essence of His Spirit

by Betsy True

I chose to read Henri Nouwen's "Love Deeply" at my father's funeral because it captures the essence of my father's spirit.

Love Deeply

Henry Nouwen

Do not hesitate to love and to love deeply. You might be afraid of the pain that deep love can cause. When those you love deeply reject you, leave you, or die, your heart will be broken. But that should not hold you back from loving deeply. The pain that comes from deep love makes your love even more fruitful. It is like a plow that breaks the ground to allow the seed to take root and grow into a strong plant. Every time you experience the pain of rejection, absence, or death, you are faced with a choice. You can become bitter and decide not to love again, or you can stand straight in your pain and let the soil on which you stand become richer and more able to give life to new seeds.

My father lived with strong conviction. He had an inner faith that drove him. When, at seventy-nine, he learned he needed dialysis, he looked into the possibility of a kidney transplant. We met with a team of kidney specialists. After they told him he was not a candidate due to his age, he stoically looked into the next type of treatment.

For five years, my father understood his dialysis treatments as his job, important work to keep him alive. In April of 2019, two months after he and my mother relocated from Worcester to Minneapolis, my father's body could no longer tolerate dialysis. And on Easter Sunday, his favorite holiday, his doctors stopped dialysis. My father was transferred to Our Lady of Peace hospice in St. Paul. He died early in the morning, his favorite time of day, on April 28, 2019.

It seems appropriate that a large group of us gathered in my father's hospital room to celebrate on Easter. Looking around the room at his children and relatives, taking us all in, he seemed so happy.

My father never gave up on life. He never said, "I'm ready to die." I think my father believed he and we could always do more to change the world and ourselves.

My father cultivated a deep spiritual life with books of poetry, religion, and literature. He wrote every day in unlined journals and in letters to friends and associates. In the end, his body gave out long before his active mind. In the hospital, he wanted to sit "straight up" in bed. He would shake his head at our apparent feeble attempts to adjust his pillows. My father wanted to be up and out in the world, despite his frailty.

My father believed in people power, the title of one his books. He also supported many people, including me, with his can-do spirit. I miss him and his positivity.

Godspeed, Dad!

Michael True

About the Author

Michael True wrote twelve books, including *An Energy Field More Intense Than War: The Nonviolent Tradition and American Literature* and *People Power: Fifty Peacemakers and Their Communities.*

Emeritus professor at Assumption University (then Assumption College), Worcester, he taught and guest-lectured at colleges and universities including Colorado College, the University of Hawaii-Manoa, and Nanjing University in China.

As a Fulbright scholar, Professor True spent time in residence at the University of Rajasthan, Jaipur, India, and Utkal University, Bhubaneswar, India.

He co-founded the Worcester County Poetry Association and the Center for Nonviolent Solutions. He served as president of the International Peace Research Association.

With Mary Pat Delaney True, his wife for more than fifty years, he had six children: Mary Laurel, Michael, John, Christopher, Betsy, and Anne.

Acknowledgments

by Anne True and Betsy True (the twins)
on behalf of the True children

The following begins a list of people who influenced, inspired, and supported our father in his effort to capture his life in a book.

He cherished his family and friends and was grateful for all of them his whole life! We gratefully acknowledge

—first and foremost, his lifelong wife and editor, Mary Pat Delaney True

—*True Commitments's* editor and publisher, Marcia Gagliardi, who met with our father several times to discuss the possibility of a memoir and has, along with the family, seen it to fruition

—the memory of our father's parents, G.H. and Agnes True; his brothers Herb and Bob; his sisters-in-law Sue True, and the late Betty Ann True

—his True nieces and nephews and to Mary Pat's clan—the Delaneys

—our father's many friends: Claire and Scott Schaeffer-Duffy, Congressman Jim McGovern, colleagues at the Center for Nonviolent Solutions, Fran Quinn, the Garrelts Family, David and Joanne O'Brien, Frank Kartheiser, and Richard Alix

—former and current colleagues at Assumption University, once Assumption College: Ann Murphy, Lucia Knowles, David Thoreen, and John Hodgen

—the Catholic intentional community, including not only the Schaeffer-Duffys but also Suzanne and Brayton Shanley of Agape, Paul Mullaney Jr., the late Bill Densmore, Mike Moran of Pax Christi, Bernie del Rosario, MD; Bob Ciottone, MD, and Arnie Hamm

— workers at DaVita Dialysis on Park Avenue in Worcester who oversaw his dialysis treatments

—the many others who buoyed his spirits

— his students, friends, and colleagues in Nanjing, China, and in India

We are excited to share *True Commitments* with you. We hope his memoir will allow you as readers to remember our father and the life he shared with and among us.

In gratitude for all of you.

Colophon

Text and captions for *True Commitments* are set in Garamond Premier Pro, an Adobe version of Garamond. Garamond is a group of many old-style serif typefaces, named for sixteenth-century Parisian engraver Claude Garamond (generally spelled as Garamont in his lifetime). Garamond-style typefaces are popular and often used, particularly for printing body text and books.

Garamond worked as an engraver of punches, the masters used to stamp matrices, the molds used to cast metal type. His designs followed the model of an influential design cut for Venetian printer Aldus Manutius by his punch cutter Francesco Griffo in 1495, and helped to establish what is now called the old-style of serif letter design, letters with a relatively organic structure resembling handwriting with a pen, but with a slightly more structured and upright design.

Titles are set in Acumin, a versatile sans-serif typeface family intended for a balanced and rational quality and designed in the twentieth century by Robert Slimbach. Solidly neo-grotesque, it performs beautifully at display sizes but also maintains an exceptional degree of sensitivity for text sizes.